edited by
len richmond and gary noguera

the
gay
liberation
book

Ramparts Press
san francisco

Library of Congress Catalog Card No. 72-85092
ISBN 0-87867-030-0 (cloth), 0-87867-031-9 (paper)

Book design by A. M. Thompson

Printed in the United States of America

"Memoirs of an Ancient Activist" from *WIN* magazine, vol. V, no. 20, November 1969.

"Confessions of an All-American Boy" originally appeared (as "Masturbation Scenes") in *Faggots and Faggotry* journal, New York, 1972.

"The Same Old Game" published as "The Gay Scene in San Francisco" in the *Berkeley Barb,* August 27, 1971.

"Games Male Chauvinists Play" from *Gay Flames,* no. 8.

"Growing Up Black and Gay" published (as "Growing Up in Chicago Black and Gay") in *Gay Sunshine,* March 1971.

"David" published in *Gay Sunshine,* March 1971.

"Off Dr. Bieber" published in the *Los Angeles Free Press,* August 14, 1970.

"The Odd Couple" from "Dear Abby," *San Francisco Chronicle,* May 1972.

"Bisexual Politics," originally "Afterthoughts," from the book *The City and the Pillar* by Gore Vidal. Copyright 1948 by E. P. Dutton & Co., Inc. rev. ed. © 1965 by E. P. Dutton & Co., Inc., and used with permission.

"My Gay Soul" from *Gay Flames,* September 11, 1970.

"A Letter from Huey" published (as "A Letter from Huey to the Revolutionary Brothers and Sisters About the Women's Liberation and Gay Liberation Movements") in the *Black Panther* newspaper.

"Father Knows Best" from *Fag Rag,* Fall 1971.

"Will You Still Need Me When I'm 64" from *Gay Sunshine.*

"Don't Call Me Brother" from the *Berkeley Barb,* April 1971.

"Breaking the Ice" from *Ecstasy,* No. 1.

"Supermen in G-Strings" from *Brother,* Spring 1972.

"Sexism in the New Army" from *Women, A Journal of Liberation.*

Gay Liberation Comics from the *Berkeley Barb,* May 14, 1971.

"Love Poem on a Theme by Walt Whitman," © 1963 by Allen Ginsberg.

Most of the people whose photos appear in this book are gay; however, not all are. One's photo appearing in this volume is not necessarily a sign of his sexual orientation.

This book is dedicated
to all our gay brothers and sisters
suffering in prisons and mental institutions

We will be returning one half of any royalties received from this book
to the gay community.

This book would not have been possible without a lot of help from our friends:

Dennis Altman (Sydney)   Morris Kight (Los Angeles)
Perry Brass (New York)   Louis Landerson (Berkeley)
Manou de Maurepas (London)   Step May (Chicago)

Also: Allen Ginsberg, Aubrey Walter, Morrie Camhi, Allen Young,
Arthur Evans, Jay Schraeter, Meher Baba, and the people at
Ramparts Press who worked so hard with us to make this book happen.

the gay liberation book

contents

part one

gay oppression

part two
gay liberation

part three

beyond gay liberation

random notes from the editors

This book is a celebration. A tribute to all gay brothers who have discovered that they are beautiful.

It was produced primarily by men, and as men of course we can't presume to speak for women. We've therefore decided to limit the focus of the book to gay men's liberation. This was an important decision for us to make. Like us, most of the contributors to this book discovered their gay pride and gay consciousness through their participation in the Gay Liberation Front. Most of these organizations were heavily male-dominated. Soon women let it be known that they did not feel comfortable at meetings where the discussions frequently dealt with the problems of gay men only. In gay liberation groups throughout the country, women often split and formed their own groups where they could deal more effectively with women's liberation without having to wade through a roomful of male egos competing for attention. (As one woman put it, "We're tired of being there to make the coffee.")

This book, then, had to be limited to what we, as gay males, knew— our own feelings and struggles—and we have tried to avoid speaking for women, gay or otherwise, in this anthology.

Many of the men who worked on this book grew up together, so to speak, in the gay liberation movement. We have worked together, marched together, fought together (and frequently fought with each other). This book has come out of that struggle. It is not of one mind. It is an imprint of many minds and hearts at this moment in time. Gay liberation is ever changing, ever disagreeing with itself, ever growing. It is the excitement of gay people breaking out of the guilt and self-hate and suicide that has been our life for so long.

The book is divided into three sections. Part 1, Gay Oppression, is the past as many of us have known it: the oppression, the prisons, the mental institutions, the fearful, perplexed parents, the compulsive cruising and impersonal sex.

Part 2 introduces the concept of Gay Liberation. The marches and rap groups. The affirmation that "Gay is Good" and "Gay is Proud." Coming out and telling our parents and friends and employers that we're gay. The new life. The breaking down of heterosexual influences on our lives—the family, the idealization of monogamous relationships, the division between sex and love.

Now that the Gay Liberation Front in all the largest cities of the U.S. has disbanded (sometimes breaking up into smaller special-interest groups), where do we go from here? Part 3, Beyond Gay Liberation, is an attempt to suggest, map out, predict what comes next. Perhaps, as some point out, it is no longer a matter of gay liberation, but of "straight liberation" as well. Heterosexuals are oppresssed too—perhaps more than gays, because often they don't see their oppression and society's manipulation of their lives as clearly as gays do. Part 3 discusses how not to be a "man"; how to get back in touch with one's feelings and the full sexuality that most have denied themselves in order to live up to society's image of being a man.

Part 3 is also a realization of what many of us have suspected for a long time: that the word "gay" is not very revolutionary any more. Shouldn't we be beyond labels? Beyond "queer" and "straight." Beyond "normal" and "abnormal." Beyond organizations, with their leaders and followers. Beyond gay liberation.

We are dealing primarily with the Gay Liberation Front and its consciousness. We did not compile this book as historians covering the entire gay movement in this country and around the world. The book does not discuss certain subcultures within the gay community. There are no articles about transvestites, or sexual sadists or masochists. Some of gay liberation's bravest and most consistently out-front advocates have been transvestites (e.g., the Christopher Street riots). And sado-masochists, it may be argued, are particularly honest about their sexual fantasies, which to some degree are shared by everyone; they contend that it is better to act out mutually enjoyed fantasies than to repress them. These two gay minorities are, however, sometimes criticized by members of the gay liberation community, who point out that transvestites, with their role-playing of stereotyped femininity, can be considered anti-woman. Sado-masochists are criticized for being anti-human, with their role-playing of a powerful person dominating a weaker one. At this moment, the issue of transvestites and sado-masochists is confused at best. Since we couldn't find any articles that really clarified the situation, we chose not to discuss these groups.

There are many gay groups and subcultures that we have left out. Some are groups that we felt were not truly into gay liberation as we have come to know it. Often they seemed more concerned with working towards a certain amount of homosexual freedom while still maintaining society's status quo. Gay liberation is a radical movement that advocates a radical change in society—its social structures, power structures, its racism and sexual dogmas. We have a commitment not just to homosexual liberation but to total human liberation.

Len Richmond
Gary Noguera
Mill Valley, California
October 1972

introduction

I first met Len and Gary at the Mill Valley bus depot across the bay
from San Francisco. We had corresponded about the book; they had
invited me to stay with them while I was revisiting the States. The
warmth and affection that they so spontaneously showed me represents in some ways the real essence of gay liberation.

For as well as the marches, the demonstrations, the "zaps" described
in this book, gay liberation is also an attempt by gay people, both men
and women, to create a new sense of community made possible by our
rejection of the socially defined concepts of what being a homosexual
means.

In the simplest terms gay liberation means a realization by gay
people that we have been not so much fucked up as fucked over. As
the social stigma of homosexuals as sick, evil, maladjusted, etc.,
ad nauseam, is replaced by an affirmation by gay people that homosexuality is as valid and valuable a form of sexual expression as is
heterosexuality—and that both are ultimately part of the same potential
for real sexual liberation—so, too, gay people feel the need to come
together in the search for a genuine form of community.

As so many of the articles in this anthology make clear, one of the worst aspects of gay oppression has been the creation among homosexuals of a schizophrenic outlook. The traditional homosexual—the stereotype the media so loves to portray, as in *The Boys in the Band*—lives two lives, seeking to divorce as completely as possible his sexual/emotional nature from his career/family commitments. Of course there have always been exceptions to this pattern, individuals prepared to risk persecution and ostracism in order to live in the open. But it is only with the emergence of gay liberation that homosexuals in large numbers have had the confidence and the pride to come out, to declare ourselves publicly and to act out our love for each other, not just in the privacy of the ghetto bars and baths but also on the streets and in public places.

The emergence of the Gay Liberation Movement in the late 1960s has been documented elsewhere; this book represents not so much a history as a collage, a collection of the anger, the pride, the joy that gay liberation has unleashed among homosexuals, not only in America but through much of the Western world. For Gary and Len have included material from other countries, in all of which, with local variations and facing somewhat different sorts of oppression, gay movements have sprung up. (There are, too, movements from which no material seems available, as well as many societies—such as the USSR and South Africa—where the organization of homosexuals, as of other oppressed groups, is totally prohibited.)

Like the women's movement, the gay movement is directed both internally and externally; that is, it seeks to attack social oppression while also altering the consciousness of gay people themselves. It is a mistake, and one that extreme proponents of revolution by consciousness are prone to make, to assume away the real oppressive nature of social institutions—schools, churches, the law, even (perhaps especially) the nuclear family as we know it. Their role in homosexual oppression needs to be understood and combatted. So too must the self-image that so many homosexuals have of ourselves, the guilt and self-doubt and inability to relate to our brothers that social oppression has laid on us. Ultimately gay liberation implies a reappraisal of society at large and of human relationships, and in a society that brands homosexuality as perverse and antisocial, the very way in which we live our lives becomes in fact political.

From this fact stem both the strengths and weaknesses of the movement. For gay liberation cannot be a nine-to-five movement, nor a weekend trip for would-be trendies. Rather it involves a new perception of one's place in society which, once experienced, leads to a redefinition of all aspects of one's everyday life. Gay liberation organizations have had a fluctuating and not always happy existence—the large Gay Liberation Fronts that existed in many American cities in 1970-71 have since collapsed. But gay liberation as an idea and as a way of relating to other gay people is increasingly spreading.

And as it spreads it affects both gays and straights—indeed it breaks down the artificial assumptions on which these distinctions are based. For it is only in a society that is frightened of and guilty about sexuality that the homo-hetero distinction is maintained with the vigor that applies in Western societies. Once men are no longer so frightened of homosexuality—and it is this fear of being branded a ''fag'' or a ''sissie'' that underlies many of the more unpleasant instances of male violence and aggression—men will be able to relate more genuinely and more lovingly, not only to each other but also to women. We may even reach a time when the sight of two men making love is not considered obscene, but when two men fighting is.

Gay liberation also means a release of genuine eroticism which offers a potential for liberation to all of us, gay or straight. The promiscuity that has been typical of homosexual life—though perhaps less typical than many, including homosexuals, have tended to assume—has often been a rather joyless, even *anti*-sexual, phenomenon, born of insecurity or guilt or loneliness, rather than a real ability to find sexual happiness. Much homosexual sex has been bad, not because it has been homosexual but because it has been accompanied by all sorts of hang-ups and neuroses. As gay liberation enables us to shed these, so too we are rediscovering the potential for human warmth and feeling that seem so absent in modern society. I can understand why one of my straight friends has told me he envies me the experience of gay liberation.

I was once asked on a TV talk show whether I wasn't afraid that gay liberation might become another cruising ground for homosexuals. My reply was that it would be better to meet one's bed partners at a movement dance than at a Mafia-run bar. Too often male homosexuals have been able to relate to each other only on the basis of either a one-night fuck or through sad parodies of the *Reader's Digest* model of conventional marriage. One of the most exciting aspects of the gay movement today is this search for new forms of relationships that fulfill more successfully our human needs for security and autonomy. This, it seems to me, is becoming a crucial question for a whole generation which has ceased to accept the traditional restraints and possessiveness of monogamous one-to-one relationships.

This anthology draws on a variety of sources and includes some writers well known in the world at large as well as many who have had important influence on the emergence of the Gay Liberation Movement. For those who wish to read further there have appeared in recent years several books expressing the views of gay liberationists, as well as a considerable number of gay liberation papers, of which the best known and most regularly appearing (in English) are probably *The Body Politic* (Toronto), *Come Together* (London), *Gay Liberator* (Detroit), and *Gay Sunshine* (San Francisco).

I do not necessarily agree with the particular selections Len and Gary have made, nor, obviously, with all of the sentiments in the various articles. In particular I regret that the division between men and women in the gay movement has meant that this anthology gives only a male perspective of gay liberation. Yet I believe that as a collection of statements of where the Gay (Men's) Liberation Movement has been, is now, and may in the future go, this book is important reading for those of us whose primary sexual identification is homosexual, as well as for those who are primarily heterosexual. By putting this book together Len and Gary have made a contribution to the continuing search for a more liberated society. They have also helped build a more genuine community than the commercial world in which most gays have heretofore moved. Ultimately, of course, we would hope for a community in which all—gay and straight, men and women, black and white, young and old—are included.

I believe this book is a small step towards this goal and hence a real part of the dialectic of liberation.

Dennis Altman
New York 1972

part one

gay oppression

Construction workers jeer gay demonstrators at police headquarters/Los Angeles,
December 1971

Paul Goodman at Los Angeles Gay Liberation Front seminar

paul goodman

memoirs of
an ancient activist

In essential ways, homosexual needs have made me a nigger. I have of
course been subject to arbitrary insult and brutality from citizens and the
police. But except for being occasionally knocked down, I have gotten off
lightly in this department, since I have a good flair for incipient trouble and
I used to be nimble on my feet. What is much more niggerizing is being
debased and abashed when it is not taken for granted that my out-going im-
pulse is my right; so I often, and maybe habitually, have the feeling that
it is not my street. I don't mean that my passes are not accepted, nobody
has a right to that; but that I'm not put down for making them. It is painful
to be frustrated, yet there is a way of rejecting someone that accords him his
right to exist and is the next best thing to accepting him; but I have rarely
enjoyed this treatment.

Allen Ginsberg and I once pointed out to Stokely Carmichael how we were niggers but he blandly put us down by saying that we could always conceal our dispositions and pass. That is, he accorded to us the same lack of imagination that one accords to niggers; we did not really exist for him. Interestingly, this dialogue was taking place on national TV, that haven of secrecy.

In general, in America, being a queer nigger is economically and professionally less disadvantageous than being a black nigger, except for a few areas like government service, where there is considerable fear and furtiveness. (In more puritanic regimes, like present-day Cuba, being queer is professionally and civilly a bad deal.) But my own experience has been very mixed. I have been fired three times because of my queer behavior or my claim to the right to it—and these are the only times I have been fired. I was fired from the University of Chicago during the early years of Hutchins, from Manumit School (an offshoot of A. J. Muste's Brookwood Labor College), and from Black Mountain College. These were highly liberal and progressive institutions, and two of them were communitarian. Frankly, my experience of radical community is that it does not tolerate my freedom. Nevertheless, I am all for community because it is a human thing, only I seem doomed to be left out.

On the other hand, my homosexual acts and the overt claim to the right to commit them have never disadvantaged me much, so far as I know, in more square institutions. I have taught at half a dozen state universities. I am continually invited, often as chief speaker, to conferences of junior high school superintendents, boards of regents, guidance counsellors, task forces on delinquency, etc., etc. I say what I think right, I make passes if there is occasion—I have even made out, which is more than I can say for conferences of SDS or Resistance. Maybe such company is so square that it does not believe, or dare to notice, my behavior; or more likely, such professional square people are more worldly and couldn't care less what you do, so long as they do not have to face anxious parents and yellow press.

On the whole, although I was desperately poor up to a dozen years ago—I brought up a family on the income of a sharecropper—I do not attribute this to being queer but to my pervasive ineptitude, truculence, and bad luck. In 1944, even the Army rejected me as "Not Military Material" (they had such a stamp), not because I was queer but because I made a nuisance of myself with pacifist action at the examination center and also had bad eyes and piles.

Curiously, however, I have been told by

Harold Rosenberg and the late Willie Poster that my sexual behavior used to do me damage in precisely the New York literary world; it kept me from being invited to advantageous parties. I don't know. What I observed in the '30s and '40s was that I was excluded from the profitable literary circles dominated by Marxists and ex-Marxists because I was kind of an anarchist. For example, I was never invited to PEN or the Committee for Cultural Freedom. Shucks! (When CCF finally got around to me at the end of the '50s, I had to turn them down because they were patently CIA.)

To stay morally alive, a nigger uses various kinds of spite, the vitality of the powerless. He can be randomly destructive; he feels he has little to lose and maybe he can prevent others from enjoying what they have. Or he can become an in-group fanatic, feeling that only his own kind are authentic and have soul. There are queers and blacks belonging to both these parties. Queers are "artists," blacks have "soul"—this is the kind of theory which, I am afraid, is self-disproving, like trying to prove you have a sense of humor. In my own case, however, being a nigger seems to inspire me to want a more elementary humanity, wilder, less structured, more variegated, and where people have some heart for one another and pay attention to

distress. That is, my plight has given energy to my anarchism, utopianism, and Gandhianism. There are blacks in this party too.

My actual political attitude is a willed reaction-formation to being a nigger. I act that "the society I live in is mine," the title of one of my books. I regard the president as my public servant whom I pay, and I berate him as a lousy worker. I am more constitutional than the Supreme Court.

In their in-group band, Gay Society, homosexuals can get to be fantastically snobbish and apolitical or reactionary, and they put on being silly like a costume. This is an understandable ego-defense—"You gotta be better than somebody"—but its payoff is very limited. When I give occasional talks to the Mattachine Society, my invariable pitch is to ally with all other libertarian groups and liberation movements, since freedom is indivisible. What is needed is not defiant pride and self-consciousness, but social space to live and breathe.

In my observation and experience, queer life has some remarkable political values. It can be profoundly democratizing, throwing together every class and group more than heterosexuality does. Its promiscuity can be a beautiful thing (but be prudent about VD). I myself have cruised rich, poor, middle class, and petit bourgeois; black, white, yellow, and brown; scholars, jocks, and dropouts; farmers, seamen, railroad men, heavy industry, light manufacturing, communications, business, and finance; civilians, soldiers and sailors, and once or twice cops. There is a kind of political meaning, I guess, in the fact that there are so many types of attractive human beings; but what is more significant is that the many functions in which I am professionally and economically engaged are not altogether cut-and-dried but retain a certain animation and sensuality. HEW in Washington and IS 210 in Harlem are not total wastes, though I talk to the wall in both. I have something to occupy me on trains and buses and during the increasingly long waits at airports. I have something to do at peace demonstrations—I am not inspirited by guitar music—though no doubt the TV files and the FBI with their little cameras have probably caught pictures of me groping somebody. For Oedipal reasons, I am usually sexually anti-Semitic, which is a drag, since there are so many fine Jews. The human characteristics which are finally important to me and can win my lasting friendship are quite simple: health, honesty, not being cruel or resentful, being willing to come across, having either sweetness or character on the face. As I reflect on it, only gross stupidity, obsessional cleanliness, racial prejudice, insanity, and being drunk or high really put me off.

In most human societies, of course, the sexual drive has been one more occasion for injustice, the rich buying the poor, males abusing females, sahibs using niggers, the adults exploiting the young. But I think this is neurotic and does not give the best satisfaction. It is normal to befriend what gives you pleasure. St. Thomas, who was a grand moral philosopher though a poor metaphysician, says that the chief human use of sex (as distinguished from the natural law of procreation) is to get to know other persons intimately, and that has been my experience.

A criticism of homosexual promiscuity is that, rather than democracy, there is an appalling superficiality of human contact, so that it is a kind of model of the mass inanity of modern urban life. I don't know if this is generally the case; just as, of the crowds who go to art galleries, I don't know who are being spoken to by the art and who are being bewildered further. "Is he interested in me or just in my skin? If I have sex with him, he will regard me as nothing" —I think this distinction is meaningless and disastrous; in fact, I follow up in exactly the opposite way, and many of my lifelong personal loyalties had sexual beginnings; but is this the rule or the exception? Given the usual coldness and fragmentation of community life at present, I have a hunch that homosexual promiscuity enriches more lives than it desensitizes. Naturally, if we had better community, we'd have better sexuality.

Sometimes it is sexual hunting first of all that brings me to a place where I meet people—e.g., I used to haunt bars on the waterfront; sometimes I am in a place for another reason and incidentally hunt—e.g., I call on my publisher and make a pass at a stock boy; sometimes these are both of a piece—e.g., I like to play handball and I am sexually interested in fellows who play handball. But these all come to the same thing, for in all situations I think, speak, and act pretty much the same. Apart from ordinary courteous adjustments of vocabulary—but not of syntax—I say the same say and do not wear different masks or find myself with a different personality. Perhaps there are two opposite reasons why I can maintain my integrity: on the one hand, I have a strong enough intellect to see how people are for real in our only world, and to be able to get in touch with them despite differences in background; on the other hand, I am likely so shut in my own preconceptions that I don't even notice glaring real obstacles that prevent communication.

How I do come on hasn't made for much success. Since I don't use my wits to manipulate, I rarely get what I want; since I don't betray my own values, I am not ingratiating; and my aristocratic egalitarianism puts people off unless they are secure enough to be aristocratically egalitarian themselves. Yet the fact that I am not phony or manipulative has also kept people from disliking or resenting me, and I usually have a good conscience. If I happen to get on with someone, there is not a lot of lies and bullshit to clear away.

Becoming a celebrity in the past few years seems to have hurt me sexually rather than helped me. For instance, decent young collegians who might like me and used to seek me out now keep a respectful distance from the distinguished man—perhaps they are now sure that I *must* be interested in their skin, not in them. And the others who seek me out just because I am well known seem to panic when it becomes clear that I don't care about that at all and I come on as myself. Of course, a simpler explanation of my worsening luck is that I'm growing older every day, probably uglier, and certainly too tired to try hard.

As a rule I don't believe in poverty and suffering as means of education, but in my case the hardship and starvation of my inept queer life have usefully simplied my notions of what a good society is. As with any other addict who cannot get an easy fix, they have kept me in close touch with material hunger.

So I cannot take the GNP very seriously, nor the status and credentials, nor grandiose technological solutions, nor ideological politics, including ideological liberation movements. For a starving person, the world has got to come across in kind. It doesn't. I have learned to have very modest goals for society and myself, things like clean air and water, green grass, children with bright eyes, not being pushed around, useful work that suits one's abilities, plain tasty food, and occasional satisfactory nooky.

A happy property of sexual acts, and perhaps especially of homosexual acts, is that they are dirty, like life: as Augustine said, *Inter urinas et feces nascimur.* In a society as middle-class, orderly, and technological as ours, it is essential to break down squeamishness, which is an important factor in what is called racism, as well as in cruelty to children and the sterile putting away of the sick and aged. Also, the illegal and catch-as-catch-can nature of many homosexual acts at present breaks down other conventional attitudes. Although I wish I could have had many a party with less apprehension and more unhurriedly—we would have enjoyed them more—yet it has been an advantage to learn that the ends of docks, the backs of trucks, back alleys, behind the stairs, abandoned bunkers on the beach, and the washrooms of trains are all adequate samples of all the space there is. For both good and bad, homosexual behavior retains some of the alarm and excitement of childish sexuality.

It is damaging for societies to check any spontaneous vitality. Sometimes it is necessary, but rarely; and certainly not homosexual acts, which, so far as I have heard, have never done any harm to anybody. A part of the hostility, paranoia, and automatic competitiveness of our society comes from the inhibition of body contact. But in a very specific way, the ban on homosexuality damages and depersonalizes the educational system. The teacher-student relation is almost always erotic; if there is a fear and to-do that it might turn into overt sex, it either lapses or becomes sick and cruel. And it is a loss that we do not have the pedagogic sexual friendships that have starred other cultures. Needless to say, a functional sexuality is incompatible with our mass school systems. This is one among many reasons they should be dismantled.

I recall when, *Growing Up Absurd* having had a number of glowing reviews, finally one irritated critic, Alfred Kazin, darkly hinted that I wrote about my Puerto Rican delinquents because I was queer for them. Naturally. How could I write a perceptive book if I didn't pay attention, and why should I pay attention to something unless, for some reason, it interested me? The motivation of most sociology, whatever it is, tends to produce worse books. I doubt that anybody would say that my observations of delinquent adolescents or of collegians in the Movement has been betrayed by infatuation. But I do care for them. (Of course, *they* might say, "With such a friend, who needs enemies?")

An evil of the hardship and danger of queer life in our society, however, as with any situation of scarcity and starvation, is that we become obsessional about it. I myself have spent far too many anxious hours of my life fruitlessly cruising, which I might have spent sauntering for nobler purposes or for nothing at all, pasturing my soul. Yet I think I have had the stamina, or stubbornness, not to let my obsession cloud my honesty. I have never praised a young fellow's bad poem because he was attractive, though of course I am then especially pleased if it is good. Best of all, of course, if he is my lover and he shows me something that I can be proud of and push.

Yes, since I began this article on a bitter note, let me end it with a happy poem I like, from *Hawkweed*:*

We have a crazy love affair,
it is wanting each other to be happy.
Since nobody else cares for that
we try to see to it ourselves.

Since everybody knows that sex
is part of love, we make love;
when that's over we return
to shrewdly plotting the other's advantage.

Today you gazed at me, that spell
is why I choose to live on.
God bless you who remind me simply
of the earth and sky and Adam.

I think of such things more than most
but you remind me simply. Man,
you make me proud to be a workman
of the Six Days, practical.

*Paul Goodman, *Hawkweed*: *Poems* (New York: Random House, 1967)

ralph hall

confessions of an all-american boy

Through the ages of innocent thirteen, annoyed fourteen, bitter fifteen, again annoyed sixteen, and angried seventeen, I was more or less into performing what I call "quickie" masturbation scenes, male nudie magazines in hand, in the storm cellar underneath our house on Main Street in upstate New York. The masturbation may have been quick, brothers, but the events leading up to the performance of the masturbatory act are quite involved, as you shall see.

Our cellar, a dismal, cold, musty place full of old bedsprings, piles of dirt and other debris, was the only place I ever felt I really wanted to be alone. I actually grew to like that cellar as a home, a home I created for myself beneath a home. No one, no one but I, ever lived in it. It had a quaint and intriguing—if somewhat surreal—atmosphere, one that invited adventure of my kind. It was a cellar with an overall desperate facade, for it was there, in that very tiny and misshapen place, that I, Ralph Daniel Hall, faggot, Social Security No. 060-36-9277, Military Serial No. 595-35-09, would for five consecutive years achieve minutes of wonderful sensual masturbation orgasms which relieved my innermost sexual frustrations, which as a result grew into various high planes of ecstasy and satisfaction, which in turn gave growth to my own autonomous freedom, the inner sanctum of my faggotry, created by myself, just for me, to spite all else ever taught me.

I was a successful but poor newspaper boy during those prime years beginning in 1958. I was also a *TV-Guide* salesman, a greeting card salesman, and an all-round door-to-door ego-builder, a flirt, a bullshit-to-make-the-quick-buck sort of soul. My travels, however objective or subjective I thought them, were remote but not extensive, being restricted to going from one end of the village to the other (but only on my mother's business passes). I usually was able to find the time to fit in all the candy stores along the way, and I guess that's why my teeth are in such bad condition now.

One store especially I remember. It was a combination news center and everything-for-everybody place. Two brothers owned and operated it. One was a passive "occasional" idiot, the other an obnoxious, silly, aggressive fool; both of them could easily sell you Fourth-of-July sparklers in the middle of winter. Summer and holidays they had a nice display, an elaborate array of timely "cockie" nudie magazines—*Playboy* (of the late fifties), *True Confessions, Strength and Health, Young Physique.*

Once a month I'd patronize that store with one asset: boldness; and one mission: to assert my right to purchase the latest and greatest issue of *Strength and Health* magazine. By the time I was sixteen, having by then outgrown the mere desire for strength and health and bodybuilding, I switched to buying the slicker, more daringly daring *Young Physique.*

I had a canvas shoulderbag in which I carried my newspapers, and when it was empty I'd wear it around (like the dandy homosexuals in the Greenwich Village scene do now), not as a symbol of or for anything, but as a grab bag—for stash. I'd cruise the newsstand and the whole store for at least half an hour before I could get up the nerve to pull the magazine off the stand, whip around, lay out my buck on the counter and, taking my magazine and shoving it into my bag, open the store door just as the next customer was coming in. When, after moments of perfect timing, I was outside, free, I could breathe again. No—not yet, no stopping, no stopping. It was just a matter of ridding myself of my paranoia: Is anyone going to come up to me, maybe one of my school friends, and want to search my bag (hey, watcha got in your bag?) and discover this filthy dirty magazine in my possession? I would try to ascertain the quickest route home to be sure no one would catch me with the goods. In a half hour's time I can walk home and be safe (if I don't look back).

The only way I could pull off the purchase of the magazine was when the passive, much nicer, "idiot" brother was tending the counter. It was to him I gave my dollar, and no one else. I trusted him. He remembered my father well. When my father was young and had the very same paper route, he'd stop at the very same store (but not, I'm sure, for the same purpose). We would talk grandly at length about my father ("How's your father doing? What's he look like now?"); it was a bore for me, but good

enough for him to be able to converse with someone many times his younger. Trust came after I had purchased my sixth issue of *Young Physique*, no longer a stranger but now one of his best regular customers.

One evening it was snowing hard, blizzard warnings were out. I decided to stop in at the store on my way home to brush off the snow and to get warm. I began talking with the passive brother—about my father of course—when suddenly in the middle of a sentence he blurted out, "Hey there, by the way—I almost forgot, young man." (What does he mean, I wondered.) He fumbled a second beneath the cigar case and came up with—yes—*Young Physique* nudie magazine, of course. That almost floored me. I knee-jerked, my face turned a passion-ripe tomato red and my mouth a blue-green dry. I was frozen silent. "Here's the new issue," he went on. "I went ahead and saved it for you." I turned my head quickly to the rack where the *Young Physique* magazines were usually located; there were none there. "Oh—gee—thanks," I said. "It was the last one left and I saved it for you," he declared, as if he had saved the day. Well, he had—at least I had something to think about going home. I reached into my pocket with my mittens still on and fumbled nervously until I was able to pull out one crumpled dollar bill. Then I skooted out the store. Zip. Zip. Zip. Wow, is it cold. Maybe I should go back in and get warm again. No, I don't want him to start talking about the magazine, although I know he won't. I had confidence in him to keep my secret and he had my trust, as I had his, that neither of us would "tell."

For many, many months thereafter this brother saved *Young Physique* for me under his cigar case and never asked further questions about my father. I was now recognized as one of his most regular customers, just like those for whom he reserved the daily and Sunday papers. He was swell, and yet it never occurred to me that he might have thought or known I was a fag or realized what I was doing with that magazine. Me, a body-builder? A one-hundred-fifteen-pound featherhead, just skin and bones, frail and ready to fall apart? Maybe he did know, and maybe he had something in common with me and kept it quiet too.

In winter I usually didn't get back home till after dark when I was carrying "the goods." I'd sneak in without (hopefully) anyone seeing me and wait until I was sure everyone in the household was upstairs. If I could hear them there, and if no one was outside in the street, I'd sneak underneath the porch (which stands on stilts), glide my body quietly over to the cellar door, carefully lift it, close it slowly over me, and make my way down the cement stairway into the dark. There I'd reach for the switch to the meager twenty-five-watt light. Finally. Safe. Mission accomplished. Done. The magazine and I were home safe.

First I'd take that damn restrictive bag off my neck and back, and open up my coat. Then I'd take the magazine out of the bag and place it at my feet. By the time I'd done all that I had a hard-on with hardly any thought or command. Then I'd make a decision: whether or not to take my cock out of my pants. I mean, I like to see my own cock hard once in a while in the privacy of my cellar world and get to hold it in my hand without fear of having someone come into the room unexpectedly and discover me holding my cock in my hand, jerking it off. Sometimes I'd pull my pants all the way down, and sometimes I'd just let my erection hang out my pants while the cold air from my mouth could be felt and seen and tasted and gulped in and out of the lump in my throat. Oh, such a great feeling. It all depended on how cold it was down in the cellar, and how frustrated and anxious I was to relieve myself, and how much time I had before I had to get back upstairs.

The magazine would be spread out in front of me. When I found a page of a guy who really turned me on, I'd cum all over.

I must have rubbed my cock too fast or too hard. I had achieved the orgasm I desired and that was that. Great. I loved it, but I wished it could last, I wished I didn't have to hurry. I didn't even feel cold standing there with my pants down and my cock dripping of sperm and my hand full of my sperm, and wow, it felt so nice to cum.

I was in love. In love with a picture of a nude guy in *Young Physique* magazine.

How incredible. Gee, what I'd go through just to be able to masturbate within one minute or two. But it was a relief to be able to share my orgasm with guys in those nudie magazines, even if I couldn't be with them in the flesh. After cumming, I'd pull my pants up, putting the new magazine with the others behind some bricks. Then I'd go upstairs and make believe I had just arrived.

nick benton
the same old game

The first time I ever knowingly walked into a gay bar was about two years ago. It happened to be one of the most popular gay bars in San Francisco, where there are over sixty such places. It was the Rendezvous, famous for its clientele of handsome young college types, a discotheque with dancing and a then rigidly enforced "no contact" rule. After working up the nerve to walk in (sure that everyone I knew would see me, and that my career in the ministry would be ruined), and wiping the sweat off my palms as I slowly climbed the stairs, I stood at the top, gazing into the dimly lit room.

"Why, this is the place," I thought, with a rush of unexpected joy. It was so much like everything else I had become used to in my twenty-five years of growing up male —and liberal. It felt comfortable. It was like a high school dance or college pub. People seemed to be acting about the same too; no one (or very few, at least) looked outlandish. It did look a little funny to see only men on the dance floor, and apparently in couples, even though there was this no-touch rule. But most of my life had been spent in places where there were only men—Cub Scouts, Boy Scouts, baseball teams, basketball teams, press boxes, barber shops, nights out with "the boys."

The only thing different about the Rendezvous was the object of the game. No— the only thing different was the name of the game.

It's like the difference between football and baseball. The object is the same—to win. You score in different ways, so the games have different names.

The name of the game in the Rendezvous was homosexuality. But the object was the same as any game—to win, to score. Only instead of crossing a goal line with a pigskin tucked under your arm, you scored by getting asked to go home with the right person, or by getting the right person to go home with you.

It didn't take me long to size up the rules.

I'd been groomed all my life on how to play games.

And mind you, I grew up straight.

Like most games, there is an offense and a defense. There's a sparring going on, and you'd better learn how to protect your goal line while moving ahead to the other team's. Timing was important, too. And position. You don't want to move in too soon— you have to be shrewd and wait for the right opening. You can't look too long at the person you want to score on, or your defense will be weakened. It's a real game, and you have to be up for it, or you will lose.

These were all the things I was sizing up my first nights in the bar.

And all the time, of course, my body was filled with the same horror that had filled it all my life. The horror that I knew I wasn't good enough for the game, that it would wipe me out.

I saw the glum uglies standing slump-shouldered in dark corners. I saw the older men with their alcoholic red eyes and pink faces guzzling bourbon at the back bar. I saw the fatties and the horse-faced with their flashy clothes, their "We Try Harder" smiles.

They were all me.

I got damned depressed my first nights in that first gay bar.

They used to call me horse-face when I was in high school.

Lovers at Gay-In/Griffith Park, Los Angeles, Summer 1971

perry brass

games
male chauvinists play

The games people play go on and on—especially in that most cruel of human games, cruising. In cruising, the hunt is on and the hunter becomes the hunted. Eventually the tension becomes so high that the whole aspect of meeting someone, the prospect of an evening of pleasure, even a lifetime of satisfaction, becomes lost in this confrontation of wills. Cruising is one of the great male chauvinist games: I can be tougher than you can be. I won't open up to you until you open up to me.

Most men try to set up their own roles in the first moments of this contest of wills. Whether the playing ground is the street, a bar, or the beach, there are always the same roles, often being played by the same men, only wearing different faces. It might be the extreme caricature of masculinity who believes it's below his masculine dignity to approach anyone else. He usually stands like a steadfast tin soldier for hours on end, wondering why this isn't his night. Next to him is the aggressive animal, the tiger stalking his way through the scene, looking at everyone but seeing no one. He is looking for the perfect fulfillment of some adolescent sex fantasy (his "type") based on his first love at the age of twelve (his first "type") and whom he expects to appear momentarily.

Then there's the verbal bully who thinks the best way to captivate his latest is to out-man him (voice three octaves below normal) or outwit him (except that you've heard it all before) or outtalk him (most of which you've heard even before he tried to outwit you).

And there are the always-with-us clothes queens (nothing below Bonwit's), size queens, body queens, height queens (nothing below six feet), race queens, blonde queens, chicken queens, astrology queens (his sign always agrees with yours), drug queens, campus queens (world's oldest frat men), muscle queens, and even queen queens.

There are the "numbers" guys who always announce that you're going to be their first of the evening. They constantly tell you what the cruising report is for every port between here, San Juan, and Dubrovnik. In other words, if you're lucky, you'll make another swell number in his address book.

And the put-up artist, who has to first off embarrass you with how you're the most beautiful thing he's ever seen (since the last most beautiful thing he's ever seen).

Or the put-down artist, who thinks he has to shake you up to get you out.

There are the fantasy creeps who stare at you all night—till you walk over to them, and then they walk away. They'd rather not know you too well.

All of these men add up to a frightening lack of self-understanding and self-confidence. They can't face up to a situation unless the roles are predefined, the definitions clearly stated. We are all too afraid to find out that the gorgeous "number" over there is just like we are inside: afraid and alone, trapped in the role he has learned how to play successfully but outgrew years ago, whether it be the gorgeous "number" or the twittering little boy of thirty.

Gay roles in the whole of society are designed by fear. Just as we act in straight society out of fear that they will discover us, we react with each other out of fear that we will discover ourselves.

It's no small wonder that because of this self-straightjacketing, many gay men develop a real hatred for men, just as many straight men hate women because of the roles they must act out. Because we are forced to live in a society that condemns us as half-men, many of us feel that we must become men and a half. This means shutting out all the real tenderness and sensitivities associated with femininity. Gay life is a gay drag when it forces a man to reject most of himself and only leaves him a shell, a mask he wears in order to live with the reality of our situation: that we are all outcasts.

We must reject what straight society has straightjacketed us with and form our own lives as real people, not just go on playing the old male-chauvinist roles left over from a dodo society. It's very simple, men. It's just a matter of getting together or falling apart.

don jackson

dachau for queers

Just north of Santa Barbara, California, travelers on U.S. Highway 101 pass what appears to be a beautiful school, its neatly chopped lawns, unobtrusive cyclone fence and majestic location giving it an air of tranquility.

It is, in fact, Atascadero State Hospital, a maximum-security facility designed to treat "sex offenders, sociopaths and cultural deviants." Most of the "patients" are plain ordinary homosexuals who, having the misfortune of being at the wrong place at the wrong time, were selected by the lottery called "morals law enforcement" to fall into the clutches of the doctors of Atascadero.

For years, disturbing rumors have circulated about what supposedly happens behind the walls of Atascadero—rumors of atrocious medical and surgical experiments similar to those of the Nazi concentration camps, of patients being turned into vegetables with experimental brain surgery, of torture and other gothic tales of horror.

Officials of the California State Department of Mental Hygiene and staff members at Atascadero have repeatedly denied the rumors, either in whole or in part.

Still the reports continue to come. They come from patients, former patients, staff members, mental health professionals, legal experts, even from doctors who have worked there.

All of the patients at Atascadero were "committed" there under the Mentally Disordered Sex Offenders Act, a California law which provides that any person who a judge feels is likely to commit a sex crime can be incarcerated in Atascadero until he has been "cured."

Under California law, all sex acts other than those between a married couple fucking (the man on top, the woman on bottom) are defined as sex crimes. In many rural counties, it is the practice to commit all suspected sex criminals to Atascadero. The MDSO law provides that such persons can be sent to Atascadero for ninety days' observation. They need not be convicted of a crime, or even arrested; thus the state avoids the "inconveniences" of a trial and preparing evidence. Once committed, the person loses all legal rights and can be kept in the hospital for life, used for medical and surgical experiments, perhaps even murdered.

Dr. Paul E. Braumwell, research chief at Atascadero, frankly summarized the Department of Mental Hygiene's view of the legality of the "treatments." "These men have no rights: If we can learn something by using them [for medical and surgical experiments], then that is a small compensation for the trouble they have caused society."

Dr. Grant H. Morris, professor of law at Wayne State University, visited Atascadero and witnessed the experiments being performed. Morris had a different view of the legality of the experiments. "The experiments were conducted in apparent violation of the Nuremberg Code, the Declaration of Helsinki and the AMA's 1966 ethical guidelines for clinical investigation," he said after his visit. The Nuremberg Code provides for an international tribunal to try government employees for "gross crimes against humanity." Many German doctors were tried by the Nuremberg Tribunal after the Second World War for similar experiments on victims in concentration camps. The AMA's ethical guidelines call for the expulsion of doctors who are "grossly unethical."

The first positive evidence of dubious happenings at Atascadero came in the spring of 1970, when a monograph by Atascadero staff members was published. The monograph, by Dr. Martin J. Reimringer, chief psychiatrist, Dr. Sterling W. Morgan, medical chief of staff, and Dr. Paul F. Braumwell, research chief of staff, told of their experiments with a drug which produces acute anxiety death panic.

According to the monograph, the drug was tried out on at least ninety unwilling "patients" at Atascadero and at least sixty-seven more at the Vacaville Medical Facility (the state prison for gays). The drug, succinylcholine (anectine), is forcibly injected into unwilling patients. It causes instant paralysis of all muscles, including those needed for breathing. The patient is taken "to the brink of death" and kept alive only through mechanical devices.

The purpose of the experiment, or "exploratory study," as the doctors called it, was to see if the drug was "effective as an agent in behavior modification." The criteria for selecting men for the experiment varied, the doctors said, but included "physical or verbal violence, deviant sexual behavior and lack of cooperation." The establishment press erroneously reported that all of the victims were "incorrigibly violent inmates." In fact, the doctors have never revealed what percentage of the victims fall into each of the four classifications, but the cases they cite indicate that many, if not most, were "verbally violent" or "sexual deviates." Near the end of the monograph, the doctors admit that many of the victims were selected merely because they were "uncooperative."

When the drug is injected, the victim loses all control of the body but retains consciousness. Respiration stops. The victim is convinced that he is going to die. Dr. Walter Nugent, chief psychiatrist at Vacaville, says, "The sensation is one of suffocation and drowning. The patient feels as if he had a heavy weight on his chest and can't get any air into his lungs. The patient feels as if he is on the brink of death." Then a technician commences to brainwash the patient, telling him how wicked he is. The doctors say that the victim might connect the behavior he is being scolded for with the feeling of dying, and so refrain from such behavior in the future.

When a copy of the monograph was leaked to the *San Francisco Chronicle,* the *Chronicle* ran a front-page exposé. "The doctors are in a tenuous legal and ethical position," the *Chronicle* commented editorially. "Both the state law and the ethical rules of the American Medical Association prohibit experiments being performed on patients without their consent." The Department of Mental Hygiene sent out a carefully worded press release to the publications which carried the Atascadero story, saying in part, "Be assured that the Department of Mental Hygiene shares your concern for the legal or illegal use of any drugs which is not in the interest of the patient. . . . The drug had been used by the research staff at Atascadero, but the use of succinylcholine has been ordered withdrawn by Dr. Lowry, director of the Department."

When the accounts of succinylcholine's use first appeared in San Francisco's Gay *Sunshine,* the story brought a flood of letters from readers, many of whom were former inmates at Atascadero. Many complained that the story concentrated too much on succinylcholine, noting that it failed to inform the readers of the other "treatments" in use at Atascadero. Several letters were from former inmates who had been subjected to electro-convulsive shock.

One particularly strong letter said that patients, including the writer, were often forcibly "choked unconscious, then dragged to the treatment room and tied down to the bed." It is important to note, he went on, that "the treatment is not given for any medical reasons, but as a punishment for violation of ward rules." The patient described the treatment as follows:

"They hit you with the first jolt, and you experience pain that you would never believe possible. At the same moment, you see what could be described as a flash of lightning. You cannot breathe, and they apply oxygen. During all this, you are in convulsions. This lasts only a few moments, but it seems like a lifetime. A few seconds after that, the pain is so severe that you pass out. About three months before I left the hospital, they made us (by threatening us with shock treatments) sign a paper saying that we have agreed to let them test drugs on us."

Among the letters was one from members of the Atascadero staff, which said that "only one or two doctors [at Atascadero] still use electro-shock therapy." The staff members seemed to imply that electro-convulsive shock is used only in a few instances; however, since it takes only five minutes to administer the treatment, "one or two doctors" would have time to turn all fourteen hundred inmates into vegetables—and electro-convulsive shock can do just that. It destroys brain tissue by sending a high-voltage electrical current through the brain. Often the victim can't even remember his name, his age, or where he went to school. In fact, most doctors say that electro-convulsive shock is a barbaric savagery worthless as treatment, and it has been outlawed in most states.

Figures as to how extensively electro-convulsive shock is used are obscured by the veil of secrecy that shrouds Atascadero. But a hint came in January of 1972 when Dr. L. J. Pope, medical superintendent of Atascadero's sister institution at Vacaville, told the *San Francisco Examiner* that the use of electro-convulsive shock has been greatly reduced, and was used on "only" 433 of Vacaville's 1400 inmates in 1972.

The next hint of outrageous happenings at Atascadero came in June 1971. Gay activist Leo Dallas, a well-known militant in the gay movement in San Francisco, wrote a story about his experiences while incarcerated at Atascadero. (Dallas had been committed to Atascadero for kissing another male in public, which the California Penal Code defines as "lewd and lascivious conduct," a felony punishable by one year to life.*) His eyewitness account of what goes on in Atascadero was published in "I Am," a gay liberation newspaper published by Emmaus House in San Francisco.

In his story, Dallas tells how Atascadero doctors tried to "cure" him of homosexuality by means of electric shocks administered to the penis. He says that technicians showed him erotic material—"but the catch is they connect an electronic device to your genitals and when you get an erection, they give you a shock to make you lose it."

Three weeks after the article was published, Dallas was arrested again for kissing a male in public—this time as he was participating in the Christopher Street West Parade in Hollywood—and was sent back to Atascadero.

Shortly after, Professor William B. Chambliss of the University of California at Santa Barbara took his class to visit Atascadero. Chambliss was so shocked by what he saw that he immediately wrote an article, published in the July/August issue of *The Humanist*.

In his article, Chambliss describes what doctors call "The Errorless Extinction of Penile Responses Therapy." The treatment consists of showing the patient pornographic slides. Each time the patient gets an erection, he is given an electric shock through a device attached to the penis; after a time the man will no longer have an erection when he sees pictures that previously caused him to be sexually stimulated. Chambliss quotes Atascadero Research Chief of Staff Braumwell as saying that the treatment is a form of aversion therapy similar to classical Pavlovian conditioning. Other doctors say that shocks damage tissue, thus destroying the ability of the penis to erect.

Chambliss responded to all this by saying: "I don't know what patients and staff are like when they are not in the institution, but judging from their behavior there, I would feel a great deal more secure about the world if the patients went home at night and the staff stayed locked up."

Among the reader mail in response to the first Atascadero story was an unsigned letter postmarked "Atascadero." "They don't use succinylcholine any more," it read, "because they have found something more horrible. It's called prolixin."

---

*California's penal code uses the "indeterminate sentence"; thus, behavior (i.e., cooperation) in prison is a major criterion for parole.—Ed.

Officials at Atascadero deny that any type of aversion-therapy drug is used there. However, Dr. L. J. Pope, medical chief at Vacaville, told a press conference that prolixin was administered to 1,093 of the 1400 inmates there during 1971.

Dr. Philip Shapiro, a psychiatrist and anti-prolixin crusader, describes prolixin as "a personality-altering drug that acts on the hypothalamus." He says that prolixin has caused irreversible brain damage resulting in Parkinson's syndrome, a condition in which the sufferer has continual, uncontrollable twitching. One large dose of prolixin is sufficient to send the victim on a three-week bad trip of terrifying delusions, mental confusion and extreme pain.

Gay activist-writer John Lastala, a former Atascadero inmate, returned to Atascadero for a visit. One inmate reported that prolixin is "extensively used" there. Lastala, in a feature story in the *Advocate,* a Los Angeles-based gay newspaper, quotes the inmate as follows:

"It seems like it's [prolixin] destroying your mind. You can't concentrate. If you're thinking three things at the same time, all those thoughts explode. If you're thinking of spaghetti, for example, the spaghetti is blown up in your mind to the size of large tubes, snaking around every which way. Your thinking is slowed down.

"It seems like your breathing is stopped. Your eyeballs move funny—feel like you're dying. The doctors tell you you're dying, and without the antidote, you die. You can't move anything. You're like a vegetable. You sweat. They tell you if you're ever caught having sex in here again, you won't get the antidote and you'll die."

Another inmate says that prolixin caused him severe physical pain for three weeks. "I became very nervous," he said; "I couldn't sit still, lay down, or walk with any steadiness. I would try to write a letter but couldn't keep my thoughts straight and my concentration was completely lost. Sleep was impossible and I was constantly tired and very confused. I lost all interest in life and I couldn't hold a conversation. . . This drug was given to me as a punishment, and not for any medical purpose."

The geographical location of Atascadero is such that it is often obscured by heavy fog. From outside the cyclone fence one can get only fleeting glimpses of the buildings during momentary clearings in the fog. And so it is with the truth about Atascadero. All that is really known are a few bits and scraps of information—an indiscreet paper by overconfident staff doctors, a few slips of the tongue in the presence of reporters, the complaints of a handful of former inmates and staff members. The full truth still lies hidden behind tight-lipped security. Yet the few shards have the unmistakable ring of truth; where there's so much smoke, there's got to be some fire.

The law permits the doctors at Atascadero to do as they wish with their charges. Their records are secret, hidden from the world. Who knows what new horrors the doctors are contemplating?

Late in 1971, Dr. Walter Freeman, often called "the father of lobotomy," told a press conference that he had "severed the frontal lobes" of a number of homosexual inmates at Atascadero. Dr. Hunter Brown of the UCLA Neuropsychiatric Institute volunteered his services free to the state—in exchange for their letting him use homosexual and habitual criminal inmates of California prisons and mental institutions for his experimental psychosurgical "cures" for homosexuality and criminal behavior. Brown admits he is already performing such surgery on sexual psychopaths but refuses to say where. But under California law, homosexuals are defined as "sexual psychopaths," and Atascadero and Vacaville are the only two institutions for homosexuals in the western United States.

There have also been remarks by several state psychiatrists indicating their belief in the theory that homosexuality results from a defect or injury to the hypothalamic nucleus of the brain. In Germany, psychosurgery is in widespread use as a cure for homosexuality. The German operation consists of inserting an electronic probe into the sex-behavior center of the brain; then it is coagulated with an electrical charge. The operation "cures" the patient of all sex drive.

"There is no doubt," says one doctor, "that homosexual tendencies can be removed by surgical procedure in the region of the sex-behavior center . . . 4 to 6 percent of the male population is infected with homosexuality. As a matter of public health policy, the treatment of such patients is at least as important as the treatment of those with organic neurological disease or neurosis."

California's anti-sex laws, among the harshest on earth, reflect the ludicrous, irrational, psychosexual views of the Victorian era. A few specific sex acts, such as sodomy, were singled out for a special statute, the penalty: life prisonment. Most sex acts, preliminaries and everything even remotely connected with sex were covered by a catch-all law which made "Lewd and Lascivious Conduct" a felony also punishable by life imprisonment. Homosexual kissing, heterosexual petting, teat kissing and fondling, solitary masturbation and a score of other sex-related acts are punishable under this statute.

Many of the inmates at Atascadero are homosexuals. A few are rapists. But a large number are persons whose sexual behavior cannot be distinguished from that of society as a whole. The only difference is that they got caught—and were made scapegoats for the sins of all.

The *San Francisco Chronicle* exposed the ludicrous depths of hypocrisy to which the State of California has fallen. They told the story of "Carl," a young man whose landlady peeked through the keyhole into Carl's bathroom and observed him masturbating. She called the police. He was convicted of "lewd and lascivious conduct" and sentenced for one year to life. He was imprisoned for twelve years.

50

joel hall

growing up black and gay

When I was about twelve I ran away from home to live with an older man. My father put out a ''missing person'' on me, and eventually they caught me. When I went to court, the judge asked my father, ''Are you aware that your son is a homosexual?'' And my father said, ''Yes.'' We had never talked about it before and that was the first time I had ever heard him refer to me as a homosexual. He was very hurt having to do it in that way. And I felt his pain; it was really a blow to him to have someone come out and ask him, ''Are you aware that your son is a homosexual?'' with his son standing right there. My father is a very honest man, so he just said, ''Yeah.'' And the judge said, ''Well, we're going to send him to Galesburg Mental Institution to try to correct his homosexuality.'' I couldn't understand anything that was happening. I had sort of an idea that I would be going to the Youth Commission, but never really accepted the fact that they'd send me to the Youth Commission for something so stupid. But they did.

The first place I was sent was to the Reception Center in Joliet. Then I was sent to St. Charles. I stayed there for about six months and got into a fight with my cottage mother. I stole some cigarettes out of her room. They gave homosexuals jobs like cleaning up. So once I took advantage of cleaning up her room and stole some cigarettes. She came down to the basement and grabbed my arm and told me not to be stealing cigarettes from her. My immediate response was to hit her; I turned around and slapped her in the face. That same night they came and handcuffed me and took me to Sheridan, because that was outrageous, you know, to slap a cottage parent.

Sheridan was a maximum security institution, with two fences with dogs between and guard towers with guns. I stayed there for three months and when I got out I went to high school where I got into more fights and was sent back to Sheridan. I was always fighting. Whenever a prisoner called me a faggot or a punk I would try to knock his brains out. They thought they knew so much about psychology and about homosexuality that they could just put us in any type of situation and we would just play along with the rules. But we really fucked up a lot of things there. We were so outlandish, you know, that we practically ran the institution. Whatever

happened, we knew about it, we had something to do with it.

I was in Sheridan the second time for a year, and I was in the hole ten months out of that year. The hole was a small cell with just a light box and a slot underneath where your food came in. And I was let out once every other day for a shower. I'd get a milk pill and a vitamin pill for breakfast, a full lunch, and then a milk pill and a vitamin pill again for dinner. The hole is where they put murderers and rapists, people they feel they can't handle. I was apparently a murderer and a rapist all combined, with my homosexuality, so they put me in the hole.

An awful lot of gay people were committing suicide, hanging themselves. They eventually gave us a building, C-8, and they put us on the fourth gallery, way up at the top. We had all the cells on the top, and even there, people would slice their wrists and refuse to do any work.

One guard was giving an awful lot of trouble. His name was Ivy, Big Ivy, and he used to really give us a lot of hell, you know, beat us up—and this was a grown-ass man, and we were fourteen, fifteen years old. So we planned to get him. First we tried getting him fired by telling lies and saying he was forcing us into homosexual behavior with him. But we couldn't get him fired because he had been there so long that everybody just wouldn't believe it. So this very good friend of mine—we used to call him Di-di—tied a sheet around his neck, and tied it up to the barred windows, and stood on top of his bed. I walked up to the door and started screaming, ''Guard, come here! Somebody's trying to hang himself!'' Ivy ran up to the door and when he opened it I pushed him in and about seven or eight gay people ran in and threw a blanket over his head and almost beat him to death and left him there. One straight brother who was very close to a lot of us—he always defended us and stuff like this—was taken to the hole; they broke both his arms and both his legs before they got him there.

My first day in Sheridan I was in the cafeteria. When you first get there, you come into this big mess hall where everybody eats. All the people eat in this big mess hall. The intake people, the new people, eat at one table. I came with two other gay brothers. And we were sitting at the table and like my name was known throughout the institution before I got there for all the shit that I'd been doing. This fellow reached over and grabbed my ass. I turned around and said, ''Don't touch me. Don't put your hands on me, 'cause you don't know me.'' And we went through this big argument. I jumped up and took my tray and threw it in his face. It was just the thing to do. We had to defend ourselves and we had these reputations to hold. Otherwise we really would have been fucked over. So I threw the tray in his face. They shot tear gas into the mess hall. The first person they ran to grab while the tear gas was settling, the first person they're carrying out to the hole, my first day there, was me. They just lifted me up and drug me out and threw me in the hole.

It's true that in jail straight men force people into homosexuality, but most of the gay people who were overt about it were all put into the same area together, or on the same tier, so we didn't have as much of that. Anyone wanting to attack one gay person would have to fight thirty or forty others first. But on the other tiers, one boy was gang-raped thirteen times, and nobody in the institution knew about it other than the inmates—he wouldn't tell the officials because he would really have been in trouble then. Finally we got him to admit his homosexuality and come over to our tier so that he wouldn't be gang-raped. There's a lot of that; I think institutions encourage things like gang rapes by keeping the tension between homosexuals and straight people there. I don't feel we should be segregated from straight men. If men are straight they won't relate to me sexually anyway, so I won't have any problems with them, right?

So I think that they encourage it by keeping us separate, and then keeping all straight men together to do their thing and calling it mass homosexual uprising and shit like that.

Every once in a while you'd hear someone was raped over on another tier. But as far as our tier was concerned, they put about forty homosexuals and about as many supposedly liberal heterosexuals, men, you know, with the role of men, and homosexuals with the role of women, on the tier together. Nobody would even utter faggot, even the guards were very careful about what they said. I was playing a role, a passive, feminine role. Had I not played a passive role and gone into the institution and been put on a straight tier, and had a homosexual relationship with one person on that tier, the whole tier would have known about it, and I would have had to have homosexual relationships with everyone on that tier because I was an overt outlet, so to speak. I think that's how a lot of the gang rapes are caused, by homosexuals going in with these superman attitudes about how butch they are and they get up there and have a relationship with one person, only it's *not* with one person, so it ends up where someone else will come up to him and proposition him or something, and he'll refuse it, and that's when he's gang-raped. I would not advise any homosexual to go in there with a superman attitude, because some of the biggest, most muscular, most macho masculine-identified men go into prison. I don't care how big you are, or how tough you are, it just happens that you'll get raped if you don't go along with the program. That's all.

At that time, I didn't identify those people on our tier who played the roles of men as homosexuals. I was into a role thing, where I was a homosexual and he was a straight man, and I related to him that way. My consciousness is entirely different now. I think that having to play those roles was extremely oppressive for many of us. In fact, that's why so many of us kept returning to the institution. Sometimes you'd see someone who left two days earlier walking right back in there. He'd go out and start prostituting, or ripping somebody off. A lot of them had intentions of being caught and going back to jail because of relationships there.

I finally graduated from grammar school in St. Charles. I took a test and somehow I passed it, and they handed me a diploma. When I got out on independent parole I went to a General Equivalency Diploma test office, and passed that too. I got a high enough score to get a scholarship to college.

College was another whole trip. What

school did for me was put me in the same type of oppressive situation, but in a more bourgeois sense, so I'd be able to get a half-assed job after I graduated, supporting the system. But in fact I wouldn't be able to get a job, because the record I had was tremendous. I was so oppressed I couldn't even see that I'd never be able to teach, I'd never be able to go through school and teach high school students or children or adults or anybody because of my criminal record. But all I was concerned with at the time was getting that diploma because that made me a part of the system, could make me some money.

I met lots of gay people in college. Most gay people in college that I know just stay in their closets and don't let anybody know. That's true for the people I knew in school, until Gay Liberation and Third World Gay Revolution came out. Those people in school were very closeted people.

Basically, I've always thought of myself as a revolutionary. When I was in jail I was a revolutionary, because I was rejecting the system. Only I was rejecting the system in a negative sense, in that I was not using my rejection constructively to turn it against the system. I've always had ideas of offing repression. As early as I can remember people have been fucking over my head, and I've always had a desire to stop people from fucking over my head.

There was quite a movement in jail between black people around Malcolm X. I was in jail when I first heard about the Black Panther party, and related to it very positively, but out of a black sense, not out of a gay sense, because they were offing gay people, verbally offing gay people, saying things like "this white man who is fucking you over is a faggot," and that was getting to me, because I was a faggot and I wasn't no white man! Finally their consciousness has changed somehow, and they've begun to relate to homosexuals as people, as a part of the people. That's when I really became a revolutionary, began to live my whole life as a revolutionary. And I could never ever consider another . . . now that I'm conscious of my oppression I could not consider any other. . . . If there was a movement to restore capitalism in this country and they offed every revolutionary, they'd have to off me too. If they restore black capitalism in this country they'd have to off me too. That's going to be oppressing me as a black, gay person.

I'm really struggling right now with developing my own gay consciousness. I think that most of the people in Third World Gay Revolution and in Gay Liberation are developing their own consciousness, and trying to relate to other consciousness-raising issues. I think that more and more third world and also white people are coming into the movement because they know they'll have a fighting chance somewhere to be gay people, whether they're third world or white, so they're going to get in there and struggle for it.

I think the people I still have the most difficulty understanding are white people. I still feel a lot of negative things about white people because of their basic racism and the extreme racism which they bring down on the black community and on black people. I really feel that straight white people bring about this whole shit. I think the thing that I'm able to see better is the gay white person's point of view, and I'm able to identify—I have something to identify with in a white gay person, in a revolutionary sense, because I'm able to see that they're oppressed as gay people also. I definitely feel that I still don't understand straight white people. I hope I will, but I don't think I'll ever be able to understand straight white people. I feel that they've created all this shit—straight white MEN in particular. Since the women's liberation movement, I've begun to relate more closely to white women, and understand their oppression, because it sort of parallels gay oppression in many ways, and I'm sort of able to understand straight white women because they're sort of able to understand gay black men, to understand their gayness. I still feel that a lot of straight white women don't understand gay black men as far as their blackness is concerned; women's liberation still has an awful lot of racism to deal with. And gay black men and gay white men have an awful lot of consciousness-raising to do before they can understand women's oppression. We have to really deal with sexism. That's really a strange thing to think about—that you're oppressed in a sexist way, and that you have to raise your own consciousness on sexism. But I can see it, because black people are consistently raising their own consciousness about their blackness, and so that's how I relate to it.

nick benton
david

"You have to be a girl before you can be a boy."

David is a young man from a farm in Iowa. Since leaving home and coming to San Francisco, he has had to hustle to survive.

David is twenty-two but he could pass for fifteen, so he had little trouble staying alive once he got into the swing of hustling. In fact, it wasn't long before David was buying fine clothes and having his hair styled. He was getting $25 to $50 a trick and could turn three or four tricks in an evening.

When I met David, he wasn't hustling as much as he had been. He was spending most of his money on grass so he could stay stoned most of the time, living alone in a room downtown ($22 per week, plus $3 extra for use of a television set).

I felt really alienated from him. When we talked, he would start to tell me about his feelings, then suddenly flip out, becoming cold and distant. It wasn't hard for me to understand why. I represented another older man to him; an older man who didn't really care about him, but just wanted his body.

And I guess I did want his body, which made me doubly uptight. It pained me because it was plain how much he desired honest affection, and how much threat of exploitation there was in every move toward affection with me.

I suppose a breakthrough came the night I came across him hustling on Market Street dressed for the part, stoned out of his mind, totally indifferent and matter-of-fact about being there. My stopping to talk with him bugged him because it was hurting his business. His eyes flitted around me in search of a business contact, a "john," while I stood there.

I told him I'd give him $10 if he came to my room just to talk. I told him I didn't have the $10 with me, but would pay him the next day. He acted impatient with me, but shrugged his shoulders and said okay. In my room, he continued to act impatient. We talked uneasily, and after a while he left. Out to hustle again, I suppose.

I felt totally shitty. Deep down I knew I was just another john, and that was why I really didn't have anything to say to him. I wished I'd never see him again. But I had promised, so I went by his room the next afternoon to give him the $10. He was stoned again, watching Popeye cartoons on TV—the way he usually spent his time when not on the street.

He turned to me and said, "Did you really come here just to give me that $10?"

"Yes," I sighed, and said goodbye and left.

That was the last I saw of him until he knocked on my door a few months later about ready to keel over from ODing on drugs. He had to find someone, and I guess I was the only person he could think of. He was afraid he was dying.

After spending a few days with me to get himself together, he went back to Iowa. Back home to parents who years before had sent him away to a mental hospital in Omaha where shock treatments did something, he fears permanently, to his brain. Back home to work seven days a week on his brother's farm. Back home to work all day, watch TV, and go to bed.

A couple of weeks ago, David came back to San Francisco. He couldn't stand Iowa any longer. His brother wouldn't even pay him for the last two weeks he worked. He spent two weeks looking for a job, but couldn't find one.

The other night, he said, he turned his first trick ($15) since coming back. He said he hated it but would have to do it more if he couldn't find a job soon.

We talked about life, about being a young man in the city. David can think—it's just that he was denied the opportunity for twenty years in the Bible Belt. After rapping awhile, he flashed: "You know, I just thought of how awful it must be to be a woman."

He talked about how being a young hustler is like being a woman, in that older men were constantly seeking to exploit him for his body. He went on and on, running the gamut of his oppression, applying it to women's oppression, and then talking about his own oppression of women. He summed it up by saying, "I guess you have to be a girl before you can be a boy."

It was a simplified way of stating the basic reality of gay liberation. A more complicated way of putting the same thing would be to say that feminine oppression (the exploitation and oppression of women, children and the feminine aspects of the male) is gay oppression—so that gay liberation is the liberation of women, children and effeminacy from the influence of the straight, macho, pig male.

David understands gay liberation, I think, better than all those bourgeois queers in gay organizations who talk about their own liberation while continuing to oppress women and younger men like David.

Gay liberation lies with the like of David, but right now David is being forced back into patterns of alienation that have destroyed so many.

allen young
gay gringo in brazil

If anyone decides to make a gay liberation button in Brazil, it won't even need words, just a picture of a deer. For reasons which no one seems to know, the word for deer (*veado*) in Portuguese is the equivalent of the English word faggot. Rio de Janeiro (population four and a half million) and São Paulo (population six million) are probably the gayest cities on the continent, but Brazilian society finds its strongest words of contempt in the vocabulary used to describe homosexuals. This is a factor, as in other societies, which teaches gay people self-hatred and is basic to gay oppression.

Take the word *veado*. In Brazil, there is a very popular numbers racket called the animal game. Bets are taken on the basis of numbers from one to twenty-five, with each number corresponding to an animal, from A to Z. This helps illiterate people—more than half of Brazil's population cannot read or write—to participate in the gambling. In the animal game, number one is the *avestruz* (ostrich), and number twenty-five is the zebra. Number twenty-four is *veado* (deer), and consequently that number has the same connotation—faggot. When a young man is twenty-four years old, he is likely to say he is twenty-three or twenty-five. Some buildings go from the twenty-third to the twenty-fifth floor.

The other most hostile word in Brazilian

slang is *bicha,* which doesn't really have any other meaning, and is the word used to describe an effeminate homosexual, or, more specifically, a guy who likes to get fucked. Its equivalent in English is a combination of femme/faggot/queen/fairy.

Brazilian gay people have their own word to describe themselves—*entendido* (*entendida* for lesbians). *Entendido* means "someone in the know" or "someone who understands." It is very much of an underground gay word, perhaps the way the word "gay" was twenty-five years ago in the U.S. The average straight Brazilian does not know this special meaning of *entendido,* since *entendido* is also used in the language in other ways. Brazilians have heard about the Gay Liberation Movement, since articles about it have appeared in their newspapers and magazines, so now, in addition to the word *entendido,* some Brazilians are using the word "gay." This is especially true among Brazil's growing freak population, which follows developments in the U.S. counterculture with special interest.

Brazil is important to me because I am enchanted with the spiritual and physical beauty of the land, the people, the tropical culture, but especially because an important part of my own development as a gay person took place there. Rio de Janeiro is a beautiful city in the tropics, with green hills rising dramatically from the blue-green ocean and the sandy curved beaches below. It was there in Rio that I first said to myself, "I am a homosexual," and it was there that I first made love with another man with a full sense of the joy of gay love. When I first arrived in Rio in July 1964, on a Fulbright scholarship, I was a very frightened closet case. Tucked away in my pocket was the name of a Brazilian psychoanalyst which a New York shrink had obtained for me from some international directory on a shelf in his office. I was going to get cured. The cure I got, however, came not from the shrink (whom I saw five days a week for three months—all in Portuguese!) but from inside myself, with the help of Rio's ubiquitous gay population. At every turn I met wonderful, warm gay people. And by spending a good deal of time looking at the near-naked people on Copacabana beach, I understood clearly just what my own sexuality really was and how foolish and repressive it was of me to continue with my psychoanalytical "cure."

Dutifully trying to be straight, I had called up a young woman I'd met at the Fulbright Commission office and asked her to go out with me. She said no to the date but invited me to a party at her place and I got involved with her crowd of friends. Within a few weeks I realized that at least two of the men in the crowd were gay, and we gradually opened up to each other. I was ready. They introduced me to the frenzied gay world of Rio—the cruising on the streets and inside movie theaters, the bars and baths, the gay world's vocabulary and customs. There was much I found shocking and distasteful—not the homosexuality but the alienation and compulsiveness which is intrinsic to that ghettoized gay world provided by straight society. But I was glad to be coming out of the closet. It was my first contact with the gay world anywhere, the first time I discovered the humanity of gay people, the first time I accepted my own sexuality fully. Quite obviously, being away from my old friends and family and so many other factors which enforced my straightness, I was in a better position to come out. (I know of many other people who have had to travel far from home in order to come out.)

I was still unwilling, however, to tell any straight friends about my gayness. The friends I chose, I should add, led the kind of double life that I was about to begin. It was another form of closetry that I was entering, though I didn't fully understand it at the time. One of my friends, João Carlos, came from a lower-middle-class family and lived in Grajaú in Rio's unfashionable north zone. He lived a lie on many fronts. He borrowed cars and told people it was his car. He said he lived in Leblon (a ritzy neighborhood in the south zone). He had a romantic relationship with a beautiful young woman, the daughter of a French diplomat. He hated himself for being poor and being gay. João Carlos saved up a supply of sleeping pills, rented a room in a cheap hotel, and, on November 1, 1964 (known in Brazil as "the day of the dead"), he ended his life. João Carlos's suicide was a heavy experience for me, coming only two months after my debut in the gay world. I felt that my own frenzied life was not so different from what his had been, and I got scared. I abstained from it all for a while to think things over, but I concluded that João Carlos was wrong and that whatever problems I was having, I was too committed to enjoying and treasuring life.

A few weeks later, I found another circle of friends, somewhat more stable and more to my liking. We all became very close, and to this day I consider some of these friends among those human beings nearest and dearest to me. They taught me much about the sense of community and closeness and the will to survive which is a basic part of gay liberation.

I spent a year in Brazil on a Fulbright, went to Chile on another scholarship (there, gay life was much more limited and difficult), and then returned to Brazil for another year to work as a teacher in the American High School. I left Brazil in July 1967, and I've always wanted to go back for a visit. I finally made it this year. I spent a total of seven weeks in Brazil this past winter, most of it in Rio, with brief visits to São Paulo and Salvador (Bahia).

The nature of my recent visit to Brazil was, of course, influenced by the fact that I had developed, in the intervening years, something of a "gay consciousness." I was openly gay in most circumstances this time. Just about the only times I had to hide my gayness, in fact, was as a favor to some of my old gay friends, all of whom were still into hiding their gayness from straight friends. This became a source of conflict between us.

It wasn't only my consciousness about not hiding that was involved. I had learned and experienced more than that from gay liberation. Several of my friends continued to speak about bichas (femmes) with incredible contempt. I objected, argued, explained, but they were set in their opinions. And then there was their view of monogamy. I was, of course, anxious to meet new people. But my friends were jealous; the presumption was that I was a sexual rival. My ideas about breaking down the separation between friends and lovers, about a more free sexuality, were threaten-ing and were not accepted.

Many younger gay people are breaking out of these molds. I met several gay freaks who had a different approach to their gayness. There was still some element of closetry in that they didn't feel 100 percent free to tell their straight friends, but they said they didn't care if their straight friends knew, that they should be able to figure it out themselves. Many of these straight freaks thought of themselves as bisexual, but generally objected to labelling. They were not into pure monogamy, nor were they into role-playing. I had the impression that these gay freaks think of themselves as quite separate from the existing gay world, even to the extent of not using the term entendido, preferring the English word "gay." Many of them had not been to any gay bars because, they said, they didn't need them. I couldn't decide how to respond to such an attitude. On the one hand, I believe that gay liberation means relating to other gay people outside of the bars, as the bars are a kind of closet. On the other hand, I felt that many of the Brazilian gay freaks were finding it easy outside the gay world because of their youth and beauty, and I also questioned the way they sought to divorce themselves from the gay world. It reminded me too much of my own feeling, which lasted for many years, that I did not want to be associated with "faggots."

Many of the straight Brazilians I knew, either freaks or intellectuals, responded well to my being openly gay with them. The heavy anti-gay attitudes in the culture, I felt, could be easily eroded. These attitudes are not so essential to Latin culture as many people seem to think, largely because Latin culture, unlike Anglo-Saxon, has never pretended that homosexuality doesn't exist. In fact, it may be more realistic or logical for Latins to accept homosexuality in the context of gay liberation than for them to attempt to eliminate homosexuality (as the Cubans are doing). I say this because the presence of at least some form of homosexuality is an integral part of Latin culture, and gay liberation offers the possibility of that presence becoming a constructive, progressive force (as opposed to the oppressive, male-chauvinist type of homosexuality permitted under fascism). But Brazilians are still pretty hung-up about sexual roles. Many Brazilians believe in the *bicha/bofe* (femme/butch) dichotomy and try to live by it. It is, of course, a reflection of the male supremacy in heterosexual relations.

The hierarchy between the masculine and the effeminate male is even clearer in Brazil than it is in the U.S. In Brazil, the average person doesn't even recognize the existence of the masculine homosexual. For example,

among working-class men, it is considered all right to fuck a *bicha*, an accomplishment of sorts, just like fucking a woman. I met a few gay guys who used to go down to the World War II memorial near downtown Rio to give blow jobs to the soldiers who stood honor guard there. The soldiers were in no way compromising their masculinity, even to their colleagues. This type of homosexuality of course usually involves no emotional commitment, at least on the part of the *bofe*. It is nevertheless a common way for Brazilian males to express themselves homosexually.

The gay world in Brazil reflects the racism of Brazilian society, though I wish at the outset to stress that the racism in the gay world is not worse than among straights; racism permeates Brazilian society. Virtually all of my Brazilian friends are white and middle-class, which is perhaps an indictment of me, but I prefer to think it has more to do with circumstances than consciousness. During my first visit to Brazil, there was one *mulato* named Renato who hung around some of the time with my friends, and the way my friends viewed Renato was, "He's *mulato*, but he's a pretty nice guy." Sometimes, rather than call him *mulato* or *preto* (black), they'd call him *moreno* (swarthy), as if that were preferable. Now, these are people who thought of themselves as being opposed to racial discrimination, who categorized themselves as leftists of some sort. One time I told my friend that I had tricked with a black guy, and he made a face, confessing to me: "I'm a racist when it comes to sex."

This year I met a black guy in a gay bar, but early in our conversation he tried to explain away his very dark skin, saying something about having been in the sun a lot: "I'm dark as a Negro." I was running my fingers through his hair (in Brazil, kinky hair is known as "bad hair") and was saying that I liked it. Then, as if he understood that I wasn't fitting the stereotype of a racist North American, he said, "I see you're not a racist. Well, it's true, I'm black, but I'm a racist anyway—I don't like Japs." The incident dismayed me, but it reminds me of so many other incidents revealing the complexity of racism in Brazil (even though Brazil's official line is that the nation exemplifies racial equality). While more than half of Brazil's population is what we would call black or brown, the predominately white gay world maintains white European beauty standards, with only the slightest allowance for African and Indian influence. While the beauty standard of the gay world in the States is also predominately white, I believe there is much more awareness of the beauty of black people. This is no doubt a result of the black liberation movement and the rejection of racism by so many North American black people, and the hard lessons so many whites have begun to learn.

In many ways, I found the situation of gay people in Brazil to be similar to that of gay people in the U.S. Brazil is a capitalist country run by a fascistic military dictatorship. The military men who run the country typify the male supremacist theme in Brazilian culture and politics. Women are totally powerless, excluded altogether not only from ruling the nation but from most aspects of Brazilian life. Within the military, so it is said, there is a good deal of homosexuality, but it is of the super-masculine militaristic type associated with male supremacy. It is totally divorced from the kind of homosexuality envisioned by the gay liberation movement. In its official pronouncements, of course, the military men pay homage to God, country and the nuclear family. Among the several movies that have been banned in Brazil is *Sunday, Bloody Sunday*. Open, proud, role-free homosexuality, or what we call gayness, is not tolerated anywhere. As for the bars, the baths, the cruising on the streets, they seem to be tolerated, at least in the biggest cities. In Salvador (population eight hundred thousand), however, the city's only gay bar was harassed by police and forced to close.

Gay people generally are compelled to stay in the closet by the same forces at work in the U.S. Many people end up on psychiatrists' couches (if they can afford it), or in mental hospitals. I heard of several people who had been murdered by Midnight Cowboy rough-trade or hustler types.

I just got a letter from a Brazilian friend who told me about a friend of his who had committed suicide, someone I had met briefly in Arembepe, a beautiful, idyllic fishing village near Salvador, on my last visit to Brazil. He plunged to his death from the Lacerda elevator, which connects the Upper City of Salvador with the Lower City, shouting, "I'm human! I'm human, too!" He'd been picked up by pigs the day before and held for twelve hours, part of an overall campaign against "hippies." In Brazil, long hair on men is still seen as effeminate, so that being a hippie and being gay are not as separate as they've become in the U.S. (I don't want to give the false impression that straight freaks in Brazil are totally open to gayness. Two gay brothers were being affectionate on the freak beach in Ipanema, a section of Rio de Janeiro, and one straight freak came up and started kicking sand on them, saying, "Get out of here! This place isn't for faggots!")

There are so many other ways, subtle and direct, that anti-gay oppression is perpetuated in Brazil. "*Vai tomar no cu*" ("Take it up your ass!") is still one of the two worst curses you can utter in Brazil. (The other terrible curse is "*Vai pela puta que pariu*"—"Go back to the whore who bore you!") These two curses illustrate the close relationship in a male-chauvinist society between the denigration of so-called passive homosexuality and the way women are categorized as either good (virgin, wife, mother) or evil (whore, slut, old maid, lesbian). There are two ways to put down a man: accuse him of being womanly, or accuse him of being the offspring of an evil woman (whore).

Though I couldn't find out for sure, I don't believe Brazil has sodomy laws as such. Cross-dressing is illegal, except for the carnival period, and, I was told, two men holding hands in a public place would be subject to arrest on some sort of morals charge. Certainly anyone who is a schoolteacher, or in any "sensitive" field, cannot be openly gay. In sum, the pattern of oppression and repression is pretty much the same as in other capitalist Western societies. Political dissidents of all types are subject to severe repression, including torture, and it is clear to me that any attempt of gay people in Brazil to organize (hold meetings, pass out leaflets, etc.) would be met with instant police repression.

If a gay group ever is formed in Brazil, I'm quite certain that it will have a very radical political perspective, that it cannot fail to make the connection between gay oppression and imperialism. I've met hundreds of Brazilian gay people and the overwhelming majority think of the United States as an imperialist country which has victimized and exploited Brazil. In fact, on many occasions I was put on the defensive for being a North American, a situation I fully understood and actually welcomed. (On my most recent visit, this did not occur so much, but that is because Brazilians now tend to assume that a young North American is an enemy of Nixon and not his emissary.) Such a gay group, however, might have problems with the traditional Brazilian left, should this left ever be allowed to function again. One gay friend, a closet case who despises his homosexuality, thinks of himself as a Marxist-Leninist and told me that gay liberation is "fascistic."

The awareness that gay people in the U.S. and elsewhere are fighting against oppression, however, is having a definite effect on the consciousness and daily lives of at least some Brazilian gay people. The pattern of sexist oppression—from the straight world and inside the gay world—is beginning to change and erode. A feminist movement is beginning to function in Brazil, looking for ways to integrate women into the process of national development. Rosemarie Muraro, one of the leading Brazilian feminists, told me that she believed that the progress of feminism would definitely break down the taboo against homosexuality in Brazil. The women of the revolutionary Puerto Rican group, the Young Lords, once wrote in a position paper that "machismo is fascism." If that is true, it is perhaps in the struggle against machismo, as carried out by Brazilian women and gay people, that Brazil's fascist regime may be overturned.

patrick haggerty

out, out, damn faggot

A very dramatic letter, in five acts of gross indignity, presented in open forum, for the edification of the Venceremos Brigade Folks.

Cast of Characters: *(In order of appearance)*
   PATRICK WIGGLEKNIFE: *a Lowly Faggot Who Fortunately Knows How to Type*
   RED BIRD McTHANE: *Great Red Bird of Right-On Revolutionary Rhetoric*
   GAIL: *Bestest Machetera in the West Witch*
   LOIS: *Woman Witch Which Saved My Ass*
   SANDY: *Witch of Blackness and Sorceress of Light*
   JACKIE: *Witch of Blood and Spitfire*
   Assorted Friends and Many More Assorted Enemies of Gay Revolution

Dear Venceremos Brigade Folks: "A Prologue Told by a Lowly Faggot, Full of Sound and Fury, Signifying Plenty."

My name is Patrick Wiggleknife. Like most of your imaginary stereotypes of theatrical people, I am a homosexual. Let me make it clear what I'm talking about. This letter is not a statement *against* anything; you, Cuba, "The Revolution," Marxism, or any of those words. It is a specific reaction (mine) on a specific topic (homosexuality) in a specific situation (the Fourth Contingent, Venceremos Brigade). I definitely have a bone to pick with you folks. I was selected to participate in the Venceremos Brigade, Fourth Contingent, by the Seattle Regional Committee. I was in Cuba from March until June of 1971, and I cut one fuck of a lot of sugar cane to "express my solidarity with the Cuban Revolution." I don't really much care at this point what your prejudices are about homosexuals or the Gay Movement. I'm not responsible for the fact that you haven't done your homework on the subject. As a bona fide homo sapiens who was a worker in a socialist society, I *assume* I have a few rights. My Marxist theoretical perspectives may not be up to snuff according to your standards, but I don't recall Karl writing about liberation for "some" oppressed peoples. I believe, if for no other reason than that I was a homosexual with the Brigade, that I can speak as someone who has experienced oppression. You folks are a little slow cleaning up your messes,

and I'm getting a little tired of smelling that mess, since it seems to have ended up in my laundry. I definitely think it's time to do the wash.

Act of Gross Indignity Number I, scene i
"I Come to Drink to the General Joy
of the Whole Table."

I arrived in Cuba bright-eyed and bushy-tailed, just itching to cut *arrobas* of that goddamn sugar cane for the liberation of all oppressed peoples. I'd like to criticize myself at this point. Optimism and naiveté have always been two of my more serious faults. I saw the Third World Caucus, the G.I. Caucus, the Women's Caucus, the Workers' Caucus and a whole list of other cauci (any similarity to the word cock-eyed is purely deliberate) develop and grow under the careful nurturing of Cuban leadership. Those people who felt that they experienced oppression due to their sexual orientation formed a caucus called the Gay Caucus. The very word "gay" inflamed every thane on the island to wield his magic knife. Suddenly evil chants appeared from nowhere in a deluge. "Divisive, unnatural, unhealthy, *maricón*, sick, cultural imperialists, bourgeois capitalistic decadence" and a host of other two-, four- and six-bit words came flying at the caucus. I wasn't quite sure what all them big words meant, but the witches whispered to me that nobody else knew what they meant either. We faggots have been kindling for witch-burnings for centuries. It was not therefore surprising that the witches I met in Cuba were my consorts, and sisters in struggle. At any rate, we rapidly got the message that particular elements in camp were interested in denying us our rights to speech and assembly.

Act I, scene ii
Enter Gail, Bestest Machetera in the West Witch
"Barefaced power swept her from my sight."

I really didn't think too much about it until a few days later while cutting cane with Gail as my partner. Gail, five foot and stout though she might be, had a reputation for being among the fastest and most hardworking cutters of us all. Why, she was known to have cut alongisde the biggest, broadest, fastest male canecutters on the Brigade and beat them to the end of the row. When she cut with me, she was invariably ahead. That's why it surprised me so to look up and see Gail's row uncut. Gail was nowhere in sight, until I looked behind me. I found my beautiful and diligent sister sitting down by herself in the cane fields, crying. "What's wrong," sez I. Sez she, "I can't stand it. They won't even treat gays like they're people." Then Gail and I had

a good cry right there, but it was a short cry because we were afraid people would see we were not cutting cane and think we were interfering with production or something. The last thing we needed was another accusation hooked on us. So we dried up and started whacking cane real fast-like. It was then that the odor of shit first hit my nostrils.

Act of Gross Indignity Number II, scene i

Enter Red Bird McThane, Great Red Bird
of Right-On Revolutionary Rhetoric

"Bring forth the Machoterrors, Children, for undaunted power should compose nothing but real males." UUGGGHHH, BBLUUUCCCKKK.

We got a few Cubans to begin listening to us and showing a few seeds of understanding. The Gay Caucus began meeting in earnest to plan for a presentation to be given in general assembly, the same as all the other caucuses in camp. Before the plans were even underway, Red Bird McThane flew into camp (under the influence of evil magic, you can be sure) and uttered a decree, dropping all over our freshly laundered work clothes. Cuban leadership stated that the Cuban delegation would not "be interested" in hearing a presentation by the Gay Caucus. When we asked, just for clarification, you understand, if this meant that no Cubans would be allowed to attend the presentation, Red Bird McThane answered, "Yes." The reasons given were: 1) Cuba had no problems regarding homosexuals. (That one really threw me. If there was no problem, why in hell did the Congress on Education and Culture spend precious time away from production to address the question? I will be talking, you can be sure, about the Congress a bit later.) 2) Gay Liberation failed to fit into either a class analysis or Marxist Theory. No one is sorrier than I that Karl was so entrenched into sexist society that he failed to predict the birth of Gay Liberation or outline the full nature of sexist oppression. Alas, he did fail, and quite miserably, too. Just ask Mrs. Karl Marx for the inside dope on that one. His failure is not surprising, seeing as how he was straight. The class analysis threw me for a loop, too. The GIs, the third worlders and the women didn't exactly have the Good Housekeeping Seal of Working-Class Solidarity embroidered on their underwear. At any rate, we didn't fit the theory you folks had rhetorated. Seeing as how Karl was a big important revolutionary theoretician and we were just a bunch of lowly faggots, it was much easier to adjust or change us than the theory, especially if all you had to do was deny us the right to a legitimate presentation. Red Bird McThane's shit was beginning to smell like out-and-out prejudice and discrimination, and that's a pretty bad smell for right-on revolutionaries to be a-dropping, now ain't it?

Nonetheless, the Gay Caucus did get itself together enough to do a really fine presentation, complete with socialist analysis, platform statement, analysis of sexist oppression, original songs, skits, and little fat Ronnie leading the group in some outrageously campy gay cheerleads. Indeed, no Cubans were present, except for two Cubans whom none of us had ever seen before. They sat quietly in the back and didn't introduce themselves or their purposes to us. At that point, I was paranoid enough, gay (ergo mentally unbalanced) enough to suspect collaboration of Red Bird McThane with counterrevolutionary magicians again. It sure did stink.

Act II, scene ii
"All the perfumes of Arabia
would not sweeten this air"

The smell was beginning to be strong enough so as to be ever-present. It was particularly acrid about five in the afternoon, Cuban sun being what it is, and lingered heavily in my nostrils, increasing in intensity every time I took another goddamn swing at that goddamn sugar cane with my goddamn machete in my goddamn blistered hand. Somehow, even Spirit of Collective Work Perfume was just a little too weak to cover more noxious odors. Splits? Division in the ranks? You bet, folks, splits aplenty. We had 'em a dime a dozen. The biggest of all was the split that started in the top of my little queer mind and ran all the way down to my gay little toes. I was being split right down the middle. I had a choice: Either be one of them studly right-on revolutionaries and shut my mouth, or continue being a little cocksucker with a mouth too big. At that point, I failed to see any real options opening up for me anywhere since Xerox wasn't hiring faggots on their executive board this year either. Yes, folks, that smell was really getting gross.

Act of Gross Indignity Number III, scene i
"The Congress was a dagger of the mind,
a false creation, proceeding from
conquistadores of oppressive Spain."

But we weren't finished yet. Not even halfway around the track. Then came the grandest, biggest, brownest shitload yet, dropped square on the heads of every queer canecutter in Cuba. This time, Red Bird McThane conspired with counterrevolutionary magicians in a fifty-gallon cauldron. He called himself the National Congress of Education and Culture. The witches stole the recipe and chanted it to me in secret. Here it is:

Double trouble in the sugar cane
stubble,
Faggot burn in Gaydom's rubble
Eye of *maricón*, blood of queer,
Add Song of Sappho, steeped in fear,
Spoon-feed Congress in dead of night,
Makes a bubbling batch of "Macho
Delight."

The hope was gone. The pass-off answers no longer worked. The contradictions blinked and blared like a fifty-foot neon sign. It was not true what we had been told. Cuba did indeed have the "Homosexual Problem." Cuba was not too busy worrying about sugar cane production and feeding the masses to deal with the question, as we had been told. The Congress did indeed deal with the question. We were sitting in the main dining hall when the announcement of the Congress came on the collective television set. Homosexuals had been pronounced "sick." New efforts toward "rehabilitation" were to be instituted, with the worst cases to be treated in rehabilitation camps. Homosexuals were to be purged from Cuban arts, were not to represent the Revolution at home or abroad. Gay Cubans in education were to be denied exposure to youth, and purged from all educational circles. New efforts in sex education would teach the children "proper" ideas of human sexuality. The whole ugly brown pile was dumped by Red Bird McThane square on every gay head in Cuba. Cubans in camp cheered and clapped, hooted and shouted hooray, with many North Americans joining in the fun. The Cubans and many North Americans, convinced that every gay Cuban was directly out of the decadent ruling class and spent all his time drawing pictures, drinking wine and putting down the Revolution (about on par with the old watermelon stereotype of blacks), were convinced that justice had been done. Meanwhile, gay sons of *macheteros* who were cutting the cane themselves were stricken with fear and terror. I know. I was there. I talked at length with those gay Cubans. I saw eighteen-, nineteen- and twenty-year-old Cuban gay men go rigid with fear. I listened to the bitter, frightened stories, to the efforts they went through to remain secret. I saw the despair, communicated in broken Spanish, about what to do (nothing), where to go (nowhere). It was apparent that the gay North Americans knew more about the problems of gay Cubans than did the Congress itself. Yet to speak was to be a cultural imperialist. We did not know Cuban culture. We did not understand the situation of gays in Cuba. We had no right to speak on the subject,

in spite of the fact that the line in Cuba was a very, very old rerun of the same shit we had been eating in the States for years, a line born and perpetrated in the minds of Western imperialists. You have been rapping that line of shit ever since 16th century imperialist Spain and before. It would appear that the oppressed Cubans have assumed the same characteristics as their former oppressors. Ruefully, an all-too-common male failing. It was definitely the same old song, eighty-seventh verse. The Congress sounded verbatim like my ninth-grade health class in Port Angeles, Washington, good old USA.

Cuba, First Free Territory in the Americas, land of my socialist dreams, crumbling into so much dust and false revolutionary rhetoric. There it was, OPPRESSION, systematic, institutionalized, as clear as a Cuban starry night, as subtle as a fucking freight train running me over again. There was no way left to hope, rationalize my coming, or even struggle with the question. Clearly, we were not wanted, nor had we ever been. "Get on down the road, faggot. We got no use for your kind here." Red Bird McThane's third, gross, repugnant indignity came down and buried us in feces.

Act IV, scene i
"Aye, into the catalogue you go
for he-men as hounds, mongrels, curs."

The Gay Caucus, pulling together with the bootstraps we didn't even have, went into closed meetings. It all becomes kind of a blur from here. What to do? What to say? Should we stay in Cuba and finish the tour? Should we go home? Clearly, we were not wanted. We should ask to leave. What about solidarity? The Revolution? The political implications of splitting? We should stay. Back and forth, back and forth we went, stay, leave, stay, leave. The fifteen people in the Gay Caucus felt every inch, every pound, every implication of the contradiction and the division at least five hundred times. We made the decision to stay. We were tired, confused, oppressed, afraid. I believe now we made the wrong decision. We should have packed up our troubles in our suitcases and split, then and there. I wish I had it to do over again. If we had left, the Venceremos Brigade would have rightfully been left to clean up every drop of shit that Red Bird McThane shat. Instead, we packed it up and carried it home with us in our heads and it's still sitting there in my dirty clothes hamper, festering and rotting. Yes, folks, we did the wrong thing. We should have told you where to get off.

Act IV, scene ii
Enter Lois, Woman Witch Which Saved My Ass

Ugly things happened to us after the announcement of the Congress. Really ugly things. I came into my tent one night after hours of deliberation in the Gay Caucus to find my entire tent filled with cold, staring straight men. My *jefe* was there, cold and staring, as were three Cubans from my work brigade. It was apparent that they had been working themselves up into a frenzy. Somehow, they had appointed one of them, a big six-foot-five tough-looking, tough-acting and tough-speaking one, to be spokesman, while the rest of them stared. Twenty silent eyes, silent mouths, as the leader proceeded to scream every indignity in the book. I was sick, puny, counter-revolutionary, disgusting, divisive, imperialistic, misinformed—the whole list, from faggot to capitalist. I endured for a while as the entire camp woke up, wide-eyed, to listen to the tirade. I began to whisper, speak, and finally shout. We would still be there shouting (or maybe I would be dead, I really don't know) if my good and braver than any of us comrade, Lois, hadn't come marching into the men's tent in her full fury of womanhood and proceeded to break the whole fiasco up. I owe Lois one. A big one. The one ounce of gay pride I had left I used feebly. I didn't leave the tent. I stayed right there in my bed all night, wide-eyed, very frightened and confused, but at least I hung on to my right to a cot to sleep in, having lost all others to the Venceremos Brigade. Oh, excuse me, I forgot one. I was granted the right to get up in the morning to face another day of sugar-cane-cutting. And folks, I did cut cane. I cut a lot of cane that day. Anger can take you down a long, long row of really tough sugar cane.

Act IV, scene iii
Enter Sandy, Witch of Blackness
and Sorceress of Light,
and Jackie, Witch of Blood and Spitfire
"Treachery—fly, good Sandy,
grab your broom and fly, fly, fly."

We had no third world people in the caucus until Sandy. All other gay third worlders had been cut by the Brigade before we got there. One was my fine friend and very revolutionary comrade Larry. He had been cut by the Seattle regional committee. It was a good thing. Larry probably would have died in Cuba. The Third World Caucus continually used our lack of third world people within the caucus to put us down, as if homosexuality were a white man's disease. Sandy was a fine black lesbian who had come to Cuba with Jackie, her long-time friend and lover. Sandy endured this whole ordeal without ever showing one sign of a crack. Her soul

has to be made of cast iron. She was offered the choice of being black or being gay. The way it came down, she could not be both. As the oppression came down heavier and heavier on the Gay Caucus, she swayed more and more of her support to us. After the Congress, she joined us. One Saturday night, the wachi pupa came. Jackie came up to me. I could tell she had had too much alcohol. She said, "I can't stand it. I'm forcing Sandy to deny her blackness because of me. What should I do?" I shrugged. What was there to do? Later that night, Jackie made an attempt on her life. She cut her wrists very severely with a razor blade. She called for me from her tent. I went. McThane wields a wicked razor. There it was, folks, blood. Running out of Jackie's arm right down onto her Cuban work boots. Talk about your contradictions! A picture is worth one hell of a lot more than ten thousand words! But then she didn't call out for you to come look at the picture, did she? Nope, folks, she did not. Nor did she call upon the revolutionary Cubans. Nor did she call out in solidarity with her class comrades. She called out for me, wherein lies the contradiction. But at that point, I was a single frightened scrawny little faggot. I couldn't do nothing except see. And I can tell you, folks, Jackie has very red blood. She was packed off to the hospital . . .

Next morning, Sandy got up and cut way

more than her share of la cana. She joined the Gay Caucus at lunch for a meeting, black as black, gay as Jeanne d'Arc, and proceeded, calmly, rationally and with patience, to rap the caucus on the knuckles for its liberal racism. Sandy, are you a witch, a woman, or a fucking mountain? Whatever you are, the saints preserve you; I fell in love with you that day, body and soul.

Act IV, scene iv
Re-enter Jackie
"But who'd 'a' thunk Witch Jackie would'a had so much blood left in her?"

Jackie was up and screaming a day later. By then we were on tour. The Cubans came to her at noon, explaining that it was again time for her "shot" of sedatives. Jackie stood up tall, teeth gnashing, and proceeded to tell them just exactly what they could do with their Cuban sedatives. Jackie is an AFDC mother of four. She's been jamming around the Lumpen School of Hard Knocks for a long time. The air turned very blue. Jackie was physically carted away, howling, screaming and fighting every step. She spent the remainder of her time in Red Bird McThane's dungeon, Havana Psychiatric Hospital, the Bastille, San Quentin, a Rehabilitation Camp, whatever in hell they are calling it these days. No matter—we all know what it is. The comments I heard about Jackie were incredible. Three times

I heard, "See, I told you homosexuality was a mental disease. Jackie is obviously unstable." Jackie joined us, righteously pissed off, for the boat ride home, about as unstable as the rock of Gibraltar. The fourth gross indignity came plummeting down. This time, we were too numb to notice. We had been wading in shit twenty feet deep for weeks. What's another ten feet or so?

Act IV, scene v
"Tomorrow, and tomorrow, and tomorrow, creeps the petty pace of the Venceremos Brigade folks."

I could go on describing one gross indignity after another, but frankly, it gets a little painful. I contacted the Seattle Regional Committee upon my return. You asked if I was going to be involved in organizing for the next Brigade. I explained that I really had to spend my energies elsewhere, but that I would very much like to meet with you once to explain my position and answer any questions. "Yes, yes," said the Brigade. "Very good idea. We'll do it as soon as possible." I requested a meeting again in August. Again in October. I'm still waiting for tomorrow. Meanwhile, you are really too busy brushing up on your Marxism-Leninism to concern yourselves with the likes of me. After all, first things first. The other day I heard via the grapevine that the gay question was raised in cadre at a Brigade meeting. The Brigade explained that no gay people had been recruited for the fifth Brigade. None applied, you said. Then came some standard shit about division, lack of class-consciousness, blah, blah, blah. My, but Red Bird McThane even knows how and where to migrate. He followed me all the way back to Seattle, and swoops in for a bull's-eye bombing real regular. And folks I'm getting really tired, weary and downright pissed off wading around in your shit.

Act V, scene i
Yet to be enacted in Birnam Wood
"Red Bird McThane shall shit no more."

Look, like I said in the beginning, I don't give a rat's ass what your position is on homosexuality, if indeed you have thought about it long enough to write a two-minute decree. It makes no difference whether homosexuality is a manifestation of Nirvana, communist love, or leprosy. That ain't the point at all, folks. The point is that you didn't treat me very nice at all when I came a-cuttin' cane. Boiled down, it's at least a case of extremely rude manners you folks have, and it works upward from there. We have a right to fuck, to congregate, express our point of view and have a list of rights as long as three hundred and fifty *VERY LONG* sugar cane rows which we cut by hand, all of which you are systematically and institutionally denying. I don't know

what revolution you folks are fighting up there, but I'm for the one that's going to make the world a better, more human place for people to live, ALL OF 'EM. Now about my laundry. Your shit has been clogging up my washing machine badly since I first heard the words "La Brigada Venceremos." I'M GETTING VERY TIRED CLEANING UP AFTER OTHER PEOPLE'S SHIT, particularly people who obviously aren't too friendly.

If you think you can resolve the contradictions by simply cutting (my, but there sure as hell is a lot of cutting around you folks . . . cut the cane, cut Jackie's arm, cut gay people from future Brigades, cut the freedom of every gay Cuban), you are sadly mistaken. That's not the way we do things down here in Birnam Wood. The witches know that McThane is gonna get his. The Gay Caucus left Jackie's very stained Cuban work boots right there in the middle of the cane row where she stopped cutting. They are buried under a two-million *arroba* pile of you-know-what. The boots are labeled, Sorry - Folks-but-Somewhere-at-the-Bottom of - This-Huge-Pile-of-Red - Bird-McThane Shit - There's-Bound-to-Be - at-Least - One Cock-Sucker. Jackie would like those boots returned to her, CLEAN!! And when Jackie says clean, she does mean spit-shined. It's the least you can do after what happened to our beautiful gay love. Pick up a shovel, folks, and start digging.

don jackson

testament of a gay militant

My earliest recollections are of a feeling of being different. When I was in the third grade, I became aware that I was different from other children. I didn't like sports and the roughhouse games boys played. I didn't like to play with girls, either. Consequently, I was an outcast. But I was not friendless. I had found three other boys who, like myself, found joy in classical music, history, drama, and precocious discussion. By the time we were in the sixth grade, our little circle had grown to six. All of us were aware of being different. None of us were aware that we were all homosexuals.

Our first few days in junior high school were filled with surprises. Students from eight different elementary schools all attended the same junior high. First came the marvelous discovery that each of the other schools had groups of "different" boys like ourselves.

Freddy, a beautiful, curly-headed boy, invited me to spend the evening listening to his records. He seduced me. I was ecstatic with joy. I've always wondered why nothing like that ever happened to me sooner.

The days that followed were the time of coming out for me and my friends. Some groups like ours had been practicing homosexuality for years. When we were brought together in junior high, all of the "different" boys were introduced into homosexuality by our more experienced brothers.

It was at about this time that it became obvious that we were outcasts. We ate at the same table in the cafeteria. We congregated together in the school yard. We were afraid to be alone. Other boys teased us and called us sissie and queers.

One night a gang of boys grabbed Freddy on the way home from school. They slashed his bicycle tires and beat him up severely for being "queer."

After that our feeling of alienation increased. We went out only in groups. The word "we" came to mean homosexual. "They" meant heterosexual. "They" were uncouth violent barbarians. "They" were stupid and insensitive, incapable of appreciating the finer things. We thought all handsome boys were gay. To our eyes, "het" boys were smaller, uglier and less developed.

When I was thirteen I discovered the Rex Theater. The Rex was a small fifty-cent movie house in a deteriorating part of town. Its little-used men's room became a meeting place for teenage homosexuals. I went there a few times and scored every time. One day, a boy slightly older than I got together with me for a mutual masturbation session in the Rex men's room. Hiding in a utility room and peering through a grille were two policemen. After watching for a while, they came charging into the room like stampeding bulls. A six-foot-four two-hundred-pound policeman grabbed me, spit on me, called me a "filthy queer," beat my head against the wall and struck me twice across the face, knocking out a tooth and cutting a large gash across my cheek with his ring. I still have the scar. Today he is chief of police. I often wonder if he still beats up thirteen-year-old boys.

A short time after, Freddy's mother caught him having sex with another boy. Freddy's parents were very religious. They belonged to some fundamentalist church where everyone spoke King James English with a southern accent. Religious pictures dotted the walls and Bibles were all over the house. When Freddy's mother wasn't playing hymns on the piano, she was going about the neighborhood carrying a Bible and religious tracts.

Freddy's parents had him committed to a "disturbed children's home." I didn't see him again until ten years later. In my senior year at college, I met a gay psychiatrist. I convinced him to come with me to visit Freddy in the state mental hospital. Freddy had been locked up in a tiny room at the children's home for four years and then transferred to the state mental hospital. At the time he was put in the home, Freddy had been physically and mentally healthy. Now, the psychiatrist said, Freddy had become permanently institutionalized as a result of being isolated and deprived of contact with other humans. The procedure in juvenile mental institutions was, and still is, to lock homosexual boys up in isolation rooms so they can't have sex and "contaminate" the "normal" inmates. The psychiatrist didn't think Freddy would ever be well. Freddy had been deprived of human relations at a crucial time of life for so long that he could never again adjust to society.

I cried out in anger when we left the hospital. I knew that the idiotic dogmas of an evil and morally bankrupt religion were responsible for destroying Freddy's life and mind. I knew that the civil and police authorities were prisoners of the superstitions and taboos internalized into the culture by cruel, inhumane and hateful religious dogmas. And from that day on, I have turned my head in loathing whenever I see anyone carrying a Bible or a crucifix. Their pathological hate and absurd taboos are responsible for what happened to Freddy and to hundreds of thousands like him.

My high school years were ones of promiscuity and joy, though marred by many hassles with "het" students and teachers. School officials knew that homosexual students congregated at certain tables in the cafeteria, and that a certain section of the school ground was gay territory. Still, they feigned ignorance. Once I went to the principal to complain about a conflict between gay and het students. I had hardly begun to talk when he cut me off, saying, "I don't want to know, I don't want to hear about it." With a pleading tone he added, "Please leave without saying another word."

That night I made my first giant stride on the path to liberation. The hypocrisy of the het world had been unveiled. The principal knew that at least 10 percent of the students were gay. He couldn't care less. What he did care about was having to acknowledge the truth. It didn't take me long to grasp that the principal's attitude is the mentality of the whole fucking heterosexual world. Most hets don't care if someone is homosexual—as long as they aren't confronted with the fact and can avoid the issue. Their anger at the admitted homosexual is the anger of hypocrisy exposed. They don't care if someone is homosexual, so long as he is a closet queen. But should anyone verbalize what everyone knows, the het world goes into an insane rage.

An editorial in the ultraconservative *National Review* states the het ethic concisely: "The homosexual who keeps his perversion a private matter should be dealt with compassionately, and allowed to live his life without undue legal interference; however, those who flaunt their perversion deserve that the full sanction of the law should fall upon them."

During my high school years I was rather frail. A serious bout with polio when I was eleven left me with the stunted, underdeveloped lungs of an eleven-year-old. It also left me with a back that aches whenever I engage in prolonged activity without back support. I knew I would have to prepare myself for a type of work that was not too exerting. Since I had an avid interest in history and social sciences, I decided to become a teacher.

My first three years of college were uneventful. I had learned to conceal my homosexuality—in fact, I prided myself on my ability to conceal it. Yet secretly, I engaged in many homosexual affairs. I had learned well the lesson given by my high school principal: as long as I did not openly confront people with my homosexuality they would accept me.

My senior year in college was a nightmare. Shortly after the fall semester began, my lover was arrested. One night John went cruising in a theater rest room. A man came into the rest room and stood staring at John, displaying obvious interest. John exhibited himself. The man was a vice cop. John was arrested on a charge of indecent exposure. John was a devout Catholic with an irrepressible compulsion to confess. He was also a writer and kept a diary which he called "The Journal." His journal contained detailed accounts of every sex act John had participated in, observed or even heard about.

My phone rang at midnight. It was the night receptionist at the central police station, a lesbian. "Two detectives just brought John in," she reported in a panicky voice; "he was arrested on a sex charge."

The gay community of the college town was still living in fear of the "Inquisition." This was an incident three years earlier in which vice officers had infiltrated the gay community to spy on it. The Inquisition ended with glaring headlines in the local paper reading, "Giant Sex Perversion Ring Broken, 352 Arrested." Those arrested included a hundred or so students, a score of professors, two doctors, a UN delegate and a member of the city council.

The reason for the panic in the receptionist's voice was evident. I went immediately to John's apartment to search for his diary. Two police cars pulled up behind me as I drove away. I knew they had come for the diary. But they were too late. I drove to a secluded orchard, saturated the three volumes with gasoline, and burned them.

The next day two plainclothesmen came charging into my political science classroom. The professor pointed me out. One knocked me out of my seat onto the floor, drew my hands behind me, and snapped on a pair of handcuffs.

They took me to the police station. One hit me in the stomach. When I bent over in pain, he hit me in the face. "Where's the journal?" he asked. I said I didn't know. "John's landlady saw you coming from his apartment last night." "I went to get my coat. I know nothing about any journal."

"We're going to fix you good, you goddamned queer," the officer responded. They locked me up in a little room. An hour later, they brought John in. He was crying and obviously in great anguish. A cop pointed at me: "Is that the man that sucked your penis?" "Yes, yes," John screamed. John was taken away. I was arrested and charged with oral copulation, a felony punishable in California by fifteen years in state prison. I was released the next day on $25,000 bail. (The bail money was furnished by a wealthy friend.)

The district attorney convinced the judge to commence a legal proceeding to commit me to Atascadero State Hospital, a state mental institution famous for experimental surgeries to "cure" homosexuality. I was sent to three psychiatrists for prolonged examinations. I told all three that John had obviously been hysterical; I most certainly was not a homosexual and had never had sex with John or any other man. In fact, I said, I had a girl friend in whom I was very interested.

My lies deceived them all. They wrote reports saying that I was definitely not homosexual. The commitment proceeding was dropped. I had paid a large sum of money to a lawyer to prepare a defense. It was never heard. Each time we appeared in court for the trial, the D.A. made a motion for a continuance (to keep me in suspense as long as possible and to cost me more money). Finally, after the sixth continuance, the judge asked the D.A. why there were so many delays. The D.A. whispered something to the judge. The judge said that the continuance would not be granted, that the case would be heard now. Whereupon the D.A. got up and said, "Your Honor, I move that the case be dismissed for lack of evidence."

I was free after eight months of anguish and ruinous expenses. I was free, but the vindictive pigs had not yet taken enough revenge to satisfy their hatred of homosexuals. They got the college administration to bring a proceeding to expel me—one month before I was to graduate. When the dean persisted in the expulsion proceeding, my lawyer threatened legal action against him and the college. Since I had not been convicted of any crime, they had no legal basis for expelling me for "immorality." Finally, the dean called me to his office and said, "All right, we're dropping the expulsion proceeding, but you will not be allowed to enroll in graduate school—not here or anywhere else in this state, ever. That's the price you have to pay for getting involved in this mess."

I was an education major. I graduated, but the final victory went to the police; my education was useless unless I could go to graduate school.

So at the age of twenty-two I went out into the world to attempt to survive. I had many strikes against me. I was physically incapacitated. I had a sex arrest record. I could not use the college as a reference, so my education was entirely worthless —and that had cost me four years of my life. I was $9,000 in debt for all the legal expenses. I was fearful, introverted and withdrawn as a result of my persecution. Yet I had an immense drive to succeed, a high intelligence and a good financial sense.

I studied for and passed an examination for a real estate broker's license. I went into business in San Francisco. It took the real estate commissioner eighteen months to find out about the trouble I had been in.

My license was revoked: I was not "of good moral repute," as required by state law.

I lived in a quiet neighborhood near San Francisco in a house I had bought from the profits of my real estate business. Fortunately I had some savings, so I was able to survive for several months while I looked for another job.

I had a possessive lover who got uptight over my promiscuity. One day he found me in bed with another man. In a fit of jealousy he knocked on the neighbors' doors to tell them I was a "queer." He wrote to my new employer telling him about the incident in college. I was fired.

Neighborhood teenage hoods began to harass me. Obscenities were written on my garage door. My car tires were slashed. A rock was thrown through my living room window. Reluctantly, I complained to the police. Six policemen came in answer to my call. Once they got inside, they tore the house apart searching for "evidence." The only "evidence" they found was an envelope full of pornography.

I was taken to the police station and questioned for over an hour. "Did you take those pictures?" "Do you show dirty pictures to neighborhood boys?" They told me a sixteen-year-old was willing to testify that I had shown him dirty pictures and sucked his cock. "We're going to let you go now," the chief detective said, "but we're coming to arrest you for child-molesting at eight o'clock tomorrow morning."

I didn't know what to do. If the police really had any evidence, why would they let me go? But many lovers had been to the house—it was possible the police had somehow coerced one of them into testifying against me.

I decided I couldn't take a chance. I packed a few essential items and loaded them in the back of my ancient station wagon. By midnight, I was on my way to San Francisco.

I arrived in San Francisco homeless, unemployed and almost broke. Fortunately, I had an old friend in town who put me up for a while. I filed for unemployment insurance. The claim was denied on the grounds that I had been fired for "immorality."

For six months I managed somehow to survive while looking for a job. It wasn't easy. Finally I found a job as a clerk with a railroad. I was worried when the railroad police fingerprinted me, but to my surprise they didn't learn about my past. Then, four years later, I made the mistake of applying to the company credit union for a loan. They ran a credit check on me and discovered my secrets. The loan was denied. I was fired again. The agent cited an Interstate Commerce Commission regulation that common carriers may employ only persons "of good moral character" as the reason for my dismissal.

After a year-long search for another job, I gave up. I haven't worked a day in eight years. I could go on and on with tales of beatings by the police, days of hunger, of being hounded and harassed, driven from town to town, but it would just be a repetition of the same old nightmare, the same old story with the same old ending. It's the story of persecution, degradation, fear and injustice spanning twenty-seven years, from 1939, when I first realized I was "different," until 1964, the year I left my last job. But it's only the first portion of my life.

The final incident that alienated me from straight society completely and forever was the 1968 murder of Kay Thomas, one of my dearest friends.

Kay was a farm boy from Oklahoma with a burning ambition to become a doctor. At the age of sixteen he set out for Dallas, wearing only a ragged T-shirt and Levis. Eight years later he graduated from the University of Texas Medical School. He came to California as a psychiatrist at Vacaville State prison. When prison officials decided to perform involuntary surgical and medical experiments on homosexual inmates, Kay quit, saying that the experiments were illegal, immoral and unethical. He went into private practice in San Francisco. He never became a financial success. He treated the poor, many of whom were gay. Few of his patients were able to pay. Hundreds of people now alive would be dead were it not for his concern.

Early in 1968, Kay's medical license was revoked. The State of California didn't approve of his lifestyle. Kay spent six months looking for a job, any kind of job, but no one would hire a queer ex-doctor. Two months later he died in the unheated garage he lived in.

I cried when I heard that Kay was dead. But tears of sorrow turned to tears of rage when I grasped that Kay had been murdered—murdered by an insane, hypocritical hatred of homosexuality.

Christians can quote the Bible—"The wages of sin is death"—and rejoice in the tragedy that has been my life. But let them not rejoice too quickly. For this time they—society—went too far. My mind was pushed to the breaking point, and I broke through. I knew the truth, and the truth has set me free. I won a final and total victory over the guilt, self-hate and fear that had haunted me all my life. I was free at last. I was cured of the loathsome disease; it had lost its hold on me forever. More important, my guilt, self-hate and fear were consumed by rage, a rage that has become the motivating force of my life. I am filled with an inexorable determination to spend the rest of my life militating to rid the world of the heinous evils produced by the perversion of morality called Christian dogma.

I have learned that my experience is not unique. I have found others who have won the same victory. That victory we came to call Gay Liberation. At first we thought Gay Liberation was part of the gay experience. But now I know it was a mistake to use the word "gay," because the religious conversion that is Liberation is for all people. Gays were the first to see that the emperor is naked, but heterosexuals still suffer from the same sexual repression, the same self-hate and fear instilled by the anti-sex taboo.

Have faith. In my heart I know that we shall overcome.

alan watts
no more armed clergymen

The problem of the homosexual in Judaeo-Christian societies is
part of the larger issue of how far the State may go in regulating
private morals, especially in a republic such as the United States,
where church and state are constitutionally separated. There is,
of course, some difficulty in drawing a precise line between public
and private morals, or between crimes with victims and crimes
without victims. It could be argued that drunkenness, drug-addiction
and gambling have victims insofar as the offender neglects or
impoverishes his or her dependents, or endangers the public while
operating a car or airplane in a state of intoxication. It could, perhaps,
be argued that one who promiscuously begets children is in some
sense a public offender. But I see no way of arguing that
certain types of sexual relationships between consenting adults can
be construed as crimes, except by religions ignorant of biology
and psychology—and not all religions are thus ignorant.

The basic superstition of such ignorant religions is that semen is equivalent to blood, and that the ejaculation of semen is, as it used to be called, "spending"—that is, losing a certain amount of psychophysical energy. Hence the notion that semen should be "spent" only in the propagation of a child, for, especially in an agricultural society, every child is an additional hand on the farm, and since many children die at or shortly after birth, the child is seen as an economic asset, and not as a liability. But before the day of microscopes no one knew that, in any ejaculation, only one spermatozoon in a million makes it. Nature, from the sexual point of view, is undoubtedly a profligate.

It was, I believe, St. Augustine of Hippo who circulated the rumor that every animal is sad after intercourse, showing how little, if anything, he knew of the experience, and his inability to distinguish between sadness and happy relaxatio₁. In my own opinion, from my own experience, the sexual orgasm is not debilitating but invigorating. It gives an almost mystical sensation of self-transcendence, of the unity of the physical body with the whole of nature, or at least of merging with one's partner. When it is over, and we have rested awhile, I am especially eager to go back to my work-play. I am convinced that happy, guiltless, and lusty intercourse stimulates the circulation and digestion, gets all the glands going, and is the best physical medicine in the world. Although some of my best friends are men, and homosexual men at that, my preference is to do this with women. But that is my own taste, and it would never occur to me to impose it on others by sermonizing, much less by requiring policemen to become armed clergymen to enforce my taste on everyone else. Any officer who voluntarily serves on a vice squad is, almost by definition, a creep who identifies sex with filth, and gets his kicks from voyeuristic snooping with intent to harm, and thus commits a crime with a victim.

Furthermore, many (though not all) men who become police or prison guards are "tough guys" who need to prove their manliness because they are secretly and guiltily homosexual, and therefore get their kinky satisfaction by being brutal to other men. I don't really like to use the word "kinky," because, when they are mutually enjoyed, all forms of sexual play are delightful. But when they are *not* mutually enjoyed, someone becomes the victim of a crime, of a violent intrusion upon his or her organism, and it might well be shown that, under our present laws, the police commit more such acts of violence than all gamblers, prostitutes, homosexuals, boozers, and drug addicts put together, except where the latter are forced into armed robbery by the high price of heroin.

Homosexuals may not like to be put in the same class as gamblers, prostitutes, boozers, and drug addicts; but this is where the law of the land has put them. And if for no other reason than promoting an honest and efficient police force, it is urgent that we write all sumptuary laws off the books: those are laws, ecclesiastical in origin, which regulate personal habits offending the moral or religious conscience of the community. The regulation of such habits may be in the province of preachers, physicians, and psychotherapists, who act by persuasion. But it is not in the province of police, who act by force. Activities of the police should be restricted to protecting life and property, directing traffic, and giving aid to people in distress.

Even if, for the sake of argument, we allow that "drink, gambling, and immorality" are physically and/or mentally injurious, it is of the essence of a free country that the community will take the risk of letting anyone go to hell in his own way, provided he does no direct violence to others. Risk is the price of freedom. The alternative is the police state, in which anything not expressly allowed is forbidden: the society of mutual mistrust. Any system in which

there is no risk, no possibility of surprise, no element of chance, no serpent about the Tree of Knowledge, no tolerance of variety, is dead, dull, self-strangling. There can be no sensation of "self" without a contrasting sensation of "other," no sensation of well-being without the contrasting apprehension of something to be avoided. This sensation of contrast is the essence of life, and wise is he who does not try to get rid of it.

Religious communities, Jewish and Christian, should realize that, by their own doctrines, no action or abstention from action is truly moral when done, or not done, for fear of punishment. If I were inclined to some form of sexual enjoyment forbidden by my religion, I would not be virtuous in avoiding it from fear of the consequences, whether they be imprisonment by the state or everlasting damnation at the Court of Heaven. A truly moral act, by these doctrines, is something done or not done for no reason other than the love of God or of other people. Only most exceptionally does intercourse between persons of the same sex or of opposite sex express hatred. The biological and psychophysical possibility of being able to communicate with other people in this particular way is a miracle, for which, whatever It is, that It should be thanked and glorified through all the endless ages of ages.

part two
gay liberation

Right: Gay Pride demonstration/Toronto, August 27, 1972
Below: Christopher Street West parade/Los Angeles 1971

Why make it sad to be gay?
Doing your thing is O.K.
Our bodies our own
So leave us alone
Go play with yourself—today.

John Lennon 1972

Gay Guerrillas perform on Santa Monica Boulevard/Los Angeles 1970

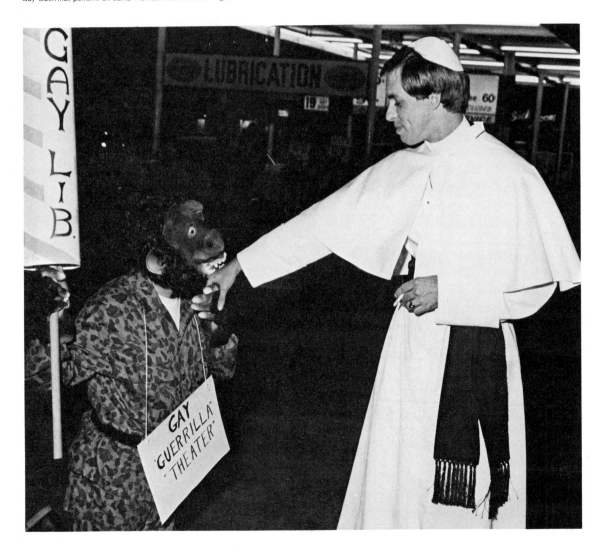

gay liberation theatre

Text of the piece written and presented by Gay Liberation Theatre, Sunday, October 6, 1969, in Lower Sproul Plaza, The University of California, Berkeley, as part of Disorientation Week.

CHORUS:
    Hello, I'm Konstantin from San Francisco.
    Hi, I'm Joel from Terre Haute.
    Hello, my name is Marshall from Jacksonville.
    Hi, I'm Karen from Pittsburgh.
    Hello, I'm Steven from Grand Rapids.
    I'm Keith from Dallas.
    My name is Jim, from Dallas.
    Hi, I'm Gary, from Minnesota.
    Hi, I'm Darwin from Bakersfield.
    My name is Lendon, from Atlanta.
    I'm Richard from Chicago.
    Hello, I'm John from Kansas City.
    I'm Dick from Riverside.
GALE: Hello, I'm Gale from Denver.

MOTHER: Are you sure you have enough underwear? Oh, and what about your winter coat? Will you be warm enough, dear? Write me and tell me what the kids are wearing. I can send whatever you need and we can go shopping together during Thanksgiving. Daddy, are you sure we're going to do the right thing? Our baby could be so easily corrupted.

FATHER: Are you sure you have enough underwear? Oh, and what about your winter coat? Will you be warm enough? Be sure you eat three square meals a day and let me know if you want me to deposit any more money in your checking account. By the way, I want you to take this. What's the matter, too old to kiss your old man? Mommy, are you sure we're doing the right thing? Our boy could be so easily corrupted.

CHORUS:
Gale will be corrupted.
Gale will be liberated.
Gale will be released.

(Dancer emerges from behind Gale, dances a brief encounter with chorus)

GALE: I'm watching, but I'm not feeling.

CHORUS: Feel.

(Dance sequence: Dancer expresses Gale's alienation and his inability to give or receive affection)

GALE: I feel funny doing that.

CHORUS: Don't do it. Or do it ten times.

MOTHER: Well, how's our baby? Our nice good boy? Been staying out of trouble? Studying hard? Dating any nice girls? Have you joined any clubs?

GALE: I keep pretty busy. I haven't had much time to commit myself and I'm glad.

FATHER: Well, how's our boy? How are you, son? Have you joined any clubs? Been dating any nice girls? Studying hard? Staying out of trouble?

GALE: I really haven't been doing much, but I've met a few interesting people.

CHORUS:
Well, how is our baby?
How's our nice boy?
Been staying out of trouble?
Studying hard?
Well, what the fuck's happening, baby?

GALE: My name is Gale, and I became aware this year.

(Dance sequence: Dancer expresses Gale's awareness and acceptance and ultimate liberation)

GALE: How can I be myself and love myself? How can I be myself and love myself unless I'm willing to be open? I want everyone to know who I am. I'm learning to love myself.

CHORUS: Who are you?

MOTHER: Gale, what are you doing home?

GALE: We're striking our classes.

MOTHER: Oh, I was afraid something like that would happen at Berkeley.

FATHER: Don't worry, the generation gap is nothing new. I raised quite a little hell when I was in college. Don't worry, he'll get it out of his system.

GALE: I've been experimenting with drugs.

MOTHER: Oh, I knew it. I knew something like that would happen in Berkeley.

FATHER: He's been mixing with the wrong people. Marijuana may or may not be any more harmful than a couple of martinis. You could be ruining your chances to get a good job, ruining your whole future.

GALE: By the way, I'm a homosexual.

MOTHER: I knew it. You're high on something right now, aren't you? Your eyes, I can tell. . . . You've been smoking pot, haven't you?

FATHER: You're a disgrace.

CHORUS:
    Disgusting
    Faggot
    Queer
    Pervert
    Fairy

GALE: Hip, black, radical, gay. Don't let them fuck you over. Be yourself.

CHORUS: Who are you?

GALE: I'm Gale when I'm naked. And I'm beautiful.—Able to leap tall buildings with a flick of the wrist . . . faster than a speeding dragster . . . more powerful than a hurtling molotov cocktail . . . the graceful, and talented . . .

—Look!!

—Up on the ceiling!

—Is it a bird?

—Is it a butterfly?

—It's . . . It's the Green Hairnet: arch-enemy of repression, champion of liberation, and screaming gay militant. Here, in a beauty salon in the heart of a downtown metropolis, mild-mannered hairdresser Bruce Hunter, otherwise known as the Green Hairnet, is doing a comb-out as our story beings.

MRS. CLYDE: So I said to her, when a marriage goes on the rocks, the rocks are usually in the mattress, but with my husband . . . (bell rings)

THE GREEN HAIRNET: Just a moment, Mrs. Clyde. (Aside) That must be the boy wonder calling me. Wonder what he wants? What wrong must I right now, what oppressed victim relieve of his suffering? Another gathering busted by the pigs? A worker discriminated against? A libido repressed? Or is Robin just horny again? I'll just slip into something more comfortable in the boys' room.

* * *

—Bruce, there's something I want to talk about. I've been thinking this over for a long time. I know there will be difficulties, and we'll have to be strong—don't you understand? I want you for my husband.
—Oh? What's he like?

* * *

—Today is the seventh day of my Pond's seven-day beauty plan and nothing's happening.

* * *

—Do you really think that the Gay Liberation Movement will produce any results?
—Perhaps not in our lifetime, but maybe in our children's, or in our children's children's . . .
—Would you mind repeating that?

* * *

—Sex will get you through times without money better than money will get you through times without dope.

* * *

—William F. Buckley wears green on Thursday.
—What does the "F" stand for?

* * *

—I know this is rather delicate, but we're good friends, and I'm afraid my Billy might grow up to be a homosexual. Of course I'm only concerned for his happiness. I'd love him just as much and try to help him . . .
—What makes you think he'll come out gay?
—Well, he takes absolutely no interest in sports; he cooks, sews, and helps me around the house . . .
—I wouldn't worry. It was the same way when I was a kid.

* * *

—Hey, didja hear the one about the traveling salesman and the farmer's son?

* * *

—Nothin' happenin' here tonight. How about if we have some fun—let's go beat some queers.
—Okay. *Oink.*

* * *

* * *

—Do you know I think my brother might be gay?
—Whistle a few bars and I'll see if I can pick it up.

* * *

—Of course we're a creative people, very talented. It's our heritage. Michelangelo, Leonardo, Oscar Wilde . . . Tab Hunter?

* * *

—Can you make me a star?
—Who did you have in mind?

* * *

—Thank you, thank you, ladies and gentlemen, and welcome this evening to another round of the Dating Game, wherein these three devastating young bachelors will compete for the dream date of a lifetime with this one. Can we begin the questioning, please?
—Number one, what are you thinking about right now?
—Oh, I guess I'm just entertaining fantasies of raping the entire Vienna Boys' Choir.
—Thank you. Number two, if I choose you, what would you like to do on our first date?

—Oh, well, uh, I'd probably, uh, take you up to my apartment and we'd, uh, smoke some grass, and then I'd probably start kissing your ear and the back of your neck and then your eyes and your ear and your mouth and we'd tear each other's clothes off and you'd help me with the zipper and I'd feel your body surging against mine and no part of our flesh would be exempt from feelings of intense pleasure and I guess I'd lick your armpit and stick my tongue in your navel and we'd probably scratch a little and do whatever you felt like and whatever you'd let me do and we'd both be breathing hard and come at the same time and experience total gratification and exhaustion.
—Thank you. Number three?

* * *

—Let it all hang out: Somebody nice might grab it.

* * *

—Did you know that a bundle of sticks is called a faggot?
—And did you know that the symbol of fascism under Mussolini was an axe in a bundle of sticks?
—Wait a minute, did you say that the symbol of fascism was an axe in a faggot?

* * *

—"And in the end . . .

—". . . The love you take . . .

—". . . Is equal to the love you make."

* * *

ANNOUNCER: And now, welcome to the continuing story of "Search for Life."

EMPLOYER: Gale, I've called you in here today because I've received several complaints about your "Gay Is Good" button. I'll have to ask you to take it off.

GALE: I won't take it off. It's what I believe in.

EMPLOYER: Then I have no recourse but to fire you. What you do in your bedroom is your own concern, but what you do on the job is our concern. I am sorry, and of course I do sympathize with your position, but that button has got to go.

GALE: Everybody knows you're gay too. Why do you have to live in a closet?

EMPLOYER: I think I've made a healthy adjustment. . . .

GALE: I don't think hiding is healthy, and I'm not going to hide.

EMPLOYER: That's your decision. This is in no way a reflection on your performance here, but someday you may learn that money is a little more impor-tant than youthful idealism, and that dis-cretion is the better part of valor. I hope there are no hard feelings, and if there's ever anything I can do for you. . . Maybe we can get together for a drink sometime.

GALE: Fuck it. I'm gay and I'm proud. And you're just plain queer.

* * *

GALE: You guys should really come to some the Gay Lib meetings; we're doing a lot of things.

RICHARD: Well, Lendon and I don't really have the time. . . .

LENDON: What sort of things are you doing?

GALE: Oh, the guerrilla theatre is perform-ing a piece in Sproul Plaza as part of Disorientation Week. We have a news-paper, and a magazine; we're circulat-ing a petition to change the fuck laws, and we have an office here in Berkeley.

LENDON: Well, we're not really into this gay militant thing. We feel that by work-ing within our community and by af-filiating ourselves with existent rev-olutionary groups we can really be of more help to the movement.

GALE: Our first objective has to be reach-ing the members of our own gay com-munity, making them recognize their own oppression and come out of hiding. Do you hide it? Are you honest about it? Do your friends know?

RICHARD: Of course our friends know, but . . .

LENDON: I mean, we're not flagrant about it—we go to no great pains to conceal it, but we don't feel we have to parade around on streetcorners or anything.

FRIEND: Hi, brothers. Hello, Gale. How's gay liberation going?

GALE: How's straight liberation going? We're getting a lot of things together. We have a guerrilla theatre group doing something for Disorientation week, a newspaper, a magazine, an office in Berkeley . . .

FRIEND: All that just to suck cocks. Really, I don't see what that has to do with the revolution. People are starving. You should be fighting the pigs with us, fighting real oppression.

GALE: Where were you when Frank Bartley was murdered here in Berkeley by the pigs?

FRIEND: I guess I didn't hear about that.

GALE: Listen, we're all working to change the world. We as a group have been oppressed. The same society that has bent your minds and fucked you over has conditioned us to stifle our sexuality. Your sexuality is at the root of your being, the core of your identity. If Ladybird had been a better lay, we might not be fucking Vietnam. Sexual repression is basic, sexual revolution is essential. We work with you. You work with us.

FRIEND: You really think it's worth it. . . . Sounds like you have a problem. Well, so long, brothers. I have an SDS meeting. Power to the people.

* * *

PRIEST: *In nomine patris et filii et spiritui sanctus, Amen.*

GALE: Forgive me, Father, for I have sinned. I went to confession last two weeks ago. These are my sins. I went to bed with a boy this week.

PRIEST: Could you clarify that a little?

GALE: I performed a sexual act with a boy.

PRIEST: How does one have sex with another boy?

GALE: I put my mouth on his penis and sucked.

PRIEST: Was this the first time that you have done this?

GALE: No, I've done it before.

PRIEST: Are you married?

GALE: To a girl?

PRIEST: What else could I be implying?

GALE: No I'm not, I'm not married.

PRIEST: Well, are you seeing any girls? Many adolescents today go through the kind of sexual confusion you describe, confusing lust with love. You know the Church's position on sexual behavior outside of marriage, particularly between members of the same sex. The holy sacrament of marriage sanctifies the sacred act of procreation. You should be seeing some nice Catholic girl . . . Have you considered the priesthood?

GALE: Yes, I did consider that, but I didn't want to drown myself. I think what you're telling me is a bunch of bullshit, and you are not my god. Come with me, my gay disciples.

(Chorus follows Gale to edge of stage)

CHORUS:
Gay is good.
Our freedom is your freedom.
If it feels good, do it.
They've got the guns but we've got the numbers.
Free the erotic angels.
Gay is Beautiful.
(Gale and Barabbas are arrested by the pigs)

PILATE: *Ecce homo.* Behold a man. People of the world, all of you, children of the universe. Which one shall be crucified, and which one shall I free to you?

CHORUS: Free them both. Both of them.

ALL: "We want our rights and we don't care how. We want a revolution NOW."

Come Together

gary alinder

off dr. bieber

Walking into the enemy's inner sanctum is an enlightening experience.
In June 1970, Gay Liberation invaded the national convention of the
American Psychiatric Association in San Francisco. We found out how
tuned out the shrinks are.

The main convention meeting looked like a refugee camp for Nixon's
silent majority. It was 99 and 44/100 percent white, straight, male,
middle-aged, upper middle class. They are the insulated ones—
separated in their immaculate garb, cars, country clubs, planes,
expensive hotels, protected from emotional involvement by a
gibberish vocabulary which translates humanity into "scientifically"
quantifiable and "objective" terms.

Oh yes, psychiatrists come in different stripes; some are right-
wingers, many are liberals, a few are radicals. But with few exceptions
they seem to be caught up in a sense of their own importance.
They expect to be listened to. They have no qualms about
male chauvinism; they've never even thought about it.

So they couldn't imagine what the woman was getting at when she took the microphone to say, "I want to know what room the women can have to meet together in, and I want to know now." The chairman went on to the next speaker. Another woman took the microphone. "I don't believe you heard—we want to know what room we can have and we want to know *now*."

A week after Kent and Cambodia, the psychiatrists had come to discuss business as usual. A caucus of radical psychiatrists described what business as usual would be: ". . . a panel about American Indians which concentrates on suicide by them rather than genocide by us . . . learning about aversion treatment for homosexuals—but not considering whether homosexuality is really a psychiatric "disease" . . . hearing about drugs, new drugs and old drugs—but not the way drugs are used to tranquilize people who are legitimately upset . . . hearing about psychiatry and law enforcement—but not about how our society uses police to oppress people and prevent change . . . discussing sexuality and abortion—but not the way sex roles are used to oppress women."

I've read psychoanalytic writing on homosexuality. They have a million theories about its "causes" and "cure." As a homosexual, I can tell you the shrinks don't know their elbows from their assholes.

I don't so much mind people playing intellectual games. But psychiatrists hold the power to inflict their games on people.

As a young homosexual you feel alone; you need answers; but there's no one to talk to. So you read books or end up under the care of a psychiatrist. You find out how sick you are. The reactionaries want to cure you through brainwashing, shock treatments, or castration. The liberals just want you to be "happy." Of course, they know homosexuality is an inferior way of life, but they have little faith in cures and encourage their patients to adapt to the "deviation." A minority of shrinks say that homosexuality falls within the "range of normality." (They said to Gay Liberation people after the sessions, "We agree with you, so what's your complaint?" One of our replies was, "You do? Why don't you tell the world? Silence is also a crime.")

One of the worst mind-pigs is Dr. Irving Bieber, professor of psychiatry at New York Medical College. Listen to Dr. Bieber:

A (male) homosexual adaptation is a result of hidden and incapacitating fears of the opposite sex . . . frequent fear of disease or injury to the genitals . . . frequently includes attempts to solve problems involving the father . . . The combination of sexual overstimulation and intense guilt and anxiety about heterosexual behavior promote precocious and compulsive activity . . . By the time the son has reached the preadolescent period, he has suffered a diffuse personality disorder . . . pathologically dependent upon his mother and beset by feelings of inadequacy, impotence and self-contempt. . . . Mothers of homosexuals are usually inadequate wives. They tend to dominate and minimize their husbands and frequently hold them more or less openly in contempt. . . . Often there is a sense of identification with a minority group which has been discriminated against. Homosexual society, however, is neither "healthy" nor "happy." Life within this society tends to reinforce, fixate and add new disturbing elements to the entrenched psychopathology of its members.*

When we heard that Bieber and company were coming to the American Psychiatric Association convention, we knew we had to be there. And we were—on the convention floor microphone:

"We've listened to you long enough; you listen to us. We're fed up with being told we're sick. You're the ones who are sick. We're gay and we're proud." Bearded Kon-

* Irving Bieber, *Homosexuality: A Psychoanalytic Study of Male Homosexuals* (New York: Random House, n.d.)

stantin running around in a bright red dress. Andy laying it on the twenty shrinks who show up for a Gay Liberation workshop. Gay guerrillas in the balcony sailing a paper airplane down to the convention floor when the delegates vote for a two-year study of violence.

Bieber is almost too good a target. His views are grotesquely reactionary; he is an old man with a pinched face and a nasal voice. A few days later we deal with Nathaniel McConaghy of Australia. Young, charming, sympathetic ("I've gone on television urging an end to discrimination against homosexuals"), he reports his "research" as part of a program entitled "Issues on Sexuality":

. . . the patient was given injections of apomorophine, after which he viewed slides of males while experiencing the resultant nausea. With aversion-relief, the patient received painful electric shocks after reading aloud phrases describing aspects of homosexual behavior. Following a series of shocks, he read aloud a phrase describing an aspect of heterosexual behavior, and this was not followed by a shock. . . .

The Veterans Memorial Auditorium is nearly full—about twenty Women's Liberation people, fifteen Gay Liberation people scattered through the three hundred psychiatrists as McConaghy begins his paper. Shouts of "vicious"; "torture"; "Get your rocks off that way?" McConaghy stops; apparently he's expected trouble.

"If you'll just listen, I'm sure you'll find I'm on your side." Intermittent heckling continues, but he completes his paper. Five minutes of discussion and the chairman announces, "This meeting is adjourned."

We are in a room of enraged psychiatrists. "They should be killed," shouts one. "Give back our air fare," shouts another.

Marie DeSantis reads from a Women's Liberation statement: "Women come to you suffering from depression. Women *ought* to feel depressed with the roles society puts on them. . . . Those roles aren't biological; those roles are learned. . . . It started when my mother threw me a doll and my brother a ball. . . ." Michael Itkin reads the Gay Liberation demands.

Anarchy. Knots of people talking loudly all over the room. Shrinks coming up asking us what we want. Finally, some discussion.

Dozens of gay brothers and sisters have told me what awful experiences they've had with shrinks. "I was in and out of mental hospitals for three years. I know how to talk their language, and they're motherfuckers," a brother told me. Another said, "When I was about nineteen, I read Bieber's book;

that set me back two or three years. Then I went to a psychiatrist who took Bieber as gospel; finally after a year I stopped."

Rather than dealing with a sick society, the shrinks deal with individual members of that society. Conform, fit in, straighten up, the shrinks tell us. Something's wrong? It's in your head. And for the privilege of getting such advice, we pay them thirty dollars an hour and more.

One of Gay Liberation's demands to the convention was the abolition of psychiatry as an oppressive tool. The more I think about it, the more I favor the abolition of psychiatry, period.

"We've known four thousand years of violence. Don't fight us, fuck us; don't shoot us, suck us."

Bruce heckling the man in the booth selling shock-treatment machines. The man demonstrates a machine which shows slides of nude males during which the male patient is painfully shocked; the next slide is of a female, the patient receives no shock.

Finally we find Dr. Bieber on a panel ("Transsexualism vs. Homosexuality: Distinct Entities?"). By this time I'm really angry. "You are the pigs who make it possible for the cops to beat homosexuals; they call us queer; you—so politely—call us sick. But it's the same thing. You make possible the beatings and rapes in prisons; you are implicated in the torturous cures perpetrated on desperate homosexuals. I've read your book, Dr. Bieber, and if that book talked about black people the way it talks about homosexuals, you'd be drawn and quartered and you'd deserve it."

Bieber answers: "I never said homosexuals were sick; what I said was that they have displaced sexual adjustment." Much laughter from us. "That's the same thing, motherfucker." He tries again. "I don't want to oppress homosexuals; I want to liberate them, to liberate them from that which is paining them—their homosexuality."

That used to be called genocide.

arthur evans

how to
zap straights

Unlike many groups that use the name "Gay Liberation Front," New York's Gay Activists' Alliance is a one-issue organization. This means that GAA is exclusively devoted to issues involving gay rights (for gay men and women *both*) and refuses to involve itself in any other issues (such as the end-the-war movement). GAA also refuses to endorse any political party or candidates for public office, thus distinguishing itself from all reformist groups that attempt to work within the party system. GAA is an action-oriented group and shuns all ideological disputes. It believes that the major task of gay liberationists is to build a strong collective sense of gay pride, gay identity, and gay culture. It disdains the idea of assimilation into the overall straight culture. To accomplish these goals, GAA advocates the use of militant (though nonviolent) confrontation tactics, as described in the following article.

Straight oppressors, watch out—gays are gonna zap you! And if you're zapped, it'll be a long time before you forget it. You're sure to be emotionally shaken. You'll get lots of bad publicity. And you may even get involved in a lengthy court suit.

The "zap" is specifically designed to do just these things. And more—to rouse closet gays from their apathy, direct gay anger toward oppressive straight institutions, and create a widespread feeling of gay identity.

Use of the zap was perfected by New York's Gay Activists' Alliance. It is a unique tactic of confrontation politics, combining the somber principles of *realpolitik* with the theatrics of high camp.

One early GAA zap was occasioned by actions of the New York City police in 1970. At this time, a wave of police repression against gays developed. Bars and baths were raided or closed down. Cruising areas were heavily patrolled. Street gays, open transvestites and gay prostitutes were ridiculed by police, arrested, and in some cases beaten.

To the chagrin of gay people, this pattern of police harassment continued well into 1970, even though John Lindsay was mayor (he had been narrowly re-elected to a second term by a coalition which included black and gay voters). GAA made numerous complaints to the mayor's office, all to no avail.

As a result of Lindsay's indifference, GAA members voted to zap him whenever he appeared in public. The first zap occurred at the seasonal opening of the Metropolitan Opera. Disguised in suit-and-tie drag (some in tuxedos), members of GAA infiltrated the crowd, stationing themselves at strategic positions in the huge, ornate lobby.

When the mayor and his wife entered the lobby just before curtain time, they were stopped dead in their tracks. Gays leapt in front of them shouting, "END POLICE HARASSMENT!" and "GAY POWER!" The huge winding staircases were filled with "respectable" people waiting to catch a glimpse of His Honor. Instead they saw a little drama of gay liberation—the mayor and his wife nonplussed, the cavernous lobby booming with gay liberation chants. (The police were slow to eject the disruptors because of their "well-dressed" appearance.)

A few days later a similar scene occurred at the opening of the Broadway play *Two by Two*. Enter the mayor and his wife—only to meet with gay confrontation. This time there was a different twist, however; Mrs. Lindsay lost her temper. She charged into the demonstrators, punching and kicking (she punched me in the chest). The police threw us out.

This reaction by the mayor's wife was

a good thing. It meant the gays had gotten to the oppressors' emotions. Previously, the gay demands had been only an abstract issue to the mayor (which he could easily ignore). Now they were forced into his private life; they were felt.

Within a few days, GAA officers were invited to meet with the deputy mayor. The police official who had originated the anti-gay activities (Seymour Pine) was transferred out of Manhattan to a petty post in Brooklyn. And the wave of police harassment subsided.

In June 1970 there was an outdoor zap directed against a member of the New York City Council. For nearly nine months, a bill that would outlaw discrimination against gays (in housing, employment, and public accommodations) had been languishing in a council committee. Its chairman, Saul Sharison, even refused to call a meeting of his committee, let alone openly push for the gay rights bill ("Intro. 475"). So GAA decided to zap Sharison hard—at his own home. Sharison lived in a huge luxury apartment building within walking distance of GAA headquarters (the latter in a rather less elegant part of town).

Every Saturday night GAA holds a huge gay dance. The weekend we decided to zap Sharison, the dance ended early so that everyone—well over a thousand—could march to Sharison's home. Dozens of police had been called out. A small contingent of gay commandos tried to force the barricades, supported by chanting from the crowd. A sit-in was staged in the building's lobby, and seven people were arrested.

All this activity produced an enormous amount of noise, which disturbed and frightened the well-to-do tenants. They turned against Sharison, deluging him with phone calls and letters and threatening to force him out of the building if anything like this occurred again. Within two weeks the harried chairman announced that his committee would meet for public hearings on Intro. 475.

Actually, the most intimidating type of zap requires far fewer people. This is the hit-and-run office disruption:

For several weeks in 1971, GAA of New York City and GAA of Long Island had been pressuring the district attorney to conduct an investigation of police harassment against gays in Suffolk County, Long Island. (For example, a solitary man had been arrested on Fire Island for "sodomy," even though it takes two to sodomize; two drunken Suffolk police had raided a gay bar and beaten the manager; and gays had been beaten and maced at a recent anti-police demonstration.) The D.A. turned a deaf ear to the gays' complaints.

The plan of the zap was to take over the office quickly, threaten the D.A. with a citizen's arrest for malfeasance, subject the chief bureaucrats to a torrent of verbal abuse and noise, and then submit peacefully to arrest. All went according to play, except that the police didn't want to arrest such a large number of people (about thirty). Instead, they shoved all the demonstrators downstairs and outside.

During the action inside, gay militants walked up to the oppressors, screaming in their faces. One militant rushed up to an assistant D.A., shouting, "Are you proud of yourself? Are you proud of yourself for oppressing homosexuals? We demand an end to police harassment! An end to entrapment! An end to sodomy laws!" The crowd of gays surrounded the oppressor, shouting with raised fists, "JUSTICE! JUSTICE! JUSTICE!" The demonstrators continued to run around the office, handing out leaflets to the employees. Sylvia, a male transvestite, took over the D.A.'s desk, answering the phone as the new county district attorney.

Zapping works. The noise, abuse and general camping-up demoralize the oppressors. Sometimes even top pigs are not too proud of the work they do. Activists can capitalize on this weakness and degrade high-ranking bureaucrats in front of their employees. The oppressors are usually taken off guard and come out looking either ridiculous or violent. When the scene is replayed on TV news, they look foolish and vulnerable.

Zaps present the oppressor with a dilemma: either capitulate, or win by resorting to violence. In either case, the Gay Liberation Movement wins—for violence against gays, especially when well-publicized, always politicizes more gays.

The ensuing publicity helped make a success of a zap that took place against New York's "Inner Circle," an exclusive, elitist collection of political reporters, press agents, politicians, and union leaders who meet from time to time to lampoon current political events. Learning that the Inner Circle planned to stage a play ridiculing the gay community and Intro. 475 at its April 1972 meeting, GAA members slipped into the ornate room in the Hilton Hotel where the Inner Circle gathers. They distributed a leaflet aimed at the press agents, criticizing them for their usually jaundiced statements and reports concerning gay news. One gay activist took over a microphone and began to speak.

At this point, several men in tuxedos (later identified as members of the Inner Circle or employees of the Hilton) attacked the gays, punching them in the face and kicking them in the groin. One member of the Uniformed Firefighters Association (and a National Golden Gloves heavyweight champion) assaulted at least two gays, knocking one unconscious (the victim later had six stitches taken around his eye). New York City policemen on the scene refused to stop the mayhem, and would not allow the gays to press charges against the attackers.

Even though the gays were beaten and thrown out, the Gay Liberation Movement won: The event subsequently received enormous publicity, even from the straight press. Private contributions poured into GAA's treasury to fund a legal suit. Prominent civil rights lawyers offered to support GAA in legal action against the attackers. Most important of all, many closet gays learned of the assault and began to think about the nature of their oppression, and what they could do about it.

Zaps are thus a form of political theater for educating the gay masses. Gays who have as yet no sense of gay pride see a zap on television or read about it in the press. First they are vaguely disturbed at the demonstrators for "rocking the boat"; eventually, when they see how the straight establishment responds, they feel anger. This anger gradually focuses on the heterosexual oppressors, and the gays develop a sense of class-consciousness. And the no-longer-closeted gays realize that assimilation into the heterosexual mainstream is no answer: gays must unite among themselves, organize their common resources for collective action, and resist.

Gay people, unite! Organize! Resist!

Gay Pride Week rally in Trafalgar
Square/London, Summer 1972

london
gay liberation front
manifesto

Throughout recorded history, oppressed groups have organized to claim their rights and obtain their needs. Homosexuals, who have been oppressed by physical violence and by ideological and psychological attacks at every level of social interaction, are at last becoming angry.

To you, our gay sisters and brothers, we say that you *are* oppressed; we intend to show you examples of the hatred and fear with which straight society relegates us to the position and treatment of sub-

humans, and to explain their basis. We will show you how we can use our righteous anger to uproot the present oppressive system with its decaying and constricting ideology, and how we, together with other oppressed groups, can start to form a new order, and a liberated lifestyle, from the alternatives which we offer.

How We're Oppressed

The oppression of gay people starts in the most basic unit of society, the family, consisting of the man in charge, a slave as his wife, and their children, on whom they

* This manifesto was produced collectively by the Manifesto Group of London GLF, fall 1971.

117

force themselves as the ideal models. The very form of the family works against homosexuality.

At some point nearly all gay people have found it difficult to cope with having the restricting images of man or woman pushed on them by their parents. It may have been from very early on, when the pressures to play with the "right" toys, and thus prove boyishness or girlishness, drove against the child's inclinations. But for all of us this is certainly a problem by the time of adolescence, when we are expected to prove ourselves socially to our parents as members of the right sex (to bring home a boy/girl friend) and to start being a "real" (oppressive) young man or a "real" (oppressed) young woman. This tension can be very destructive.

The fact that gay people notice they are different from other men and women in the family situation causes them to feel ashamed, guilty and failures. How many of us have really dared be honest with our parents? How many of us have been thrown out of home? How many of us have been pressured into marriage, sent to psychiatrists, frightened into sexual inertia, ostracized, banned, emotionally destroyed —all by our parents?

Family experiences may differ widely, but in their education all children confront a common situation. Schools reflect the values of society in their formal academic curriculum, and reinforce them in their morality and discipline. Boys learn competitive, ego-building sports, and have more opportunity in science, whereas girls are given emphasis on domestic subjects, needlework, etc. Again, we gays were all forced into a rigid sex role which we did not want or need. It is quite common to discipline children for behaving in a way like the opposite sex; degrading titles like "sissy" and "tomboy" are widely used.

In the content of education, homosexuality is generally ignored, even where we know it exists, as in history and literature. Even sex education, which has been considered a new liberal dynamic of secondary schooling, proves to be little more than an extension of Christian morality. Homosexuality is again either ignored, or attacked with moralistic warnings and condemnations. The adolescent recognizing his or her homosexuality might feel totally alone in the world, or a pathologically sick wreck.

. . . our whole legal structure is supposedly based on Christianity, whose archaic and irrational teachings support the family and marriage as the only permitted condition for sex. Gay people have been attacked as abominable and sinful since the beginning of both Judaism and Christianity, and even if today the Church is playing down these strictures on homosexuality, its new ideology is that gay people are pathetic objects for sympathy.

The press, radio, television and advertising are used as reinforcements against us, and make possible the control of people's thoughts on an unprecedented scale. Entering everyone's home, affecting everyone's life, the media controllers, all representatives of the rich, male-controlled world, can exaggerate or suppress whatever information suits them.

Under different circumstances, the media might not be the weapon of a small minority. The present controllers are therefore dedicated defenders of things as they stand. Accordingly, the images of people which they transmit in their pictures and words do not subvert, but support society's image of "normal" man and woman. It follows that we are characterized as scandalous, obscene perverts; as rampant, wild sex-monsters; as pathetic, doomed and compulsive degenerates, while the truth is blanketed under a conspiracy of silence.

Antihomosexual morality and ideology, at every level of society, manifest themselves in a special vocabulary for denigrating gay people. There is abuse like "pansy," "fairy," "lesbo" to hurl at men and women who can't or won't fit stereotyped preconceptions. There are words like "sick," "bent" and "neurotic" for destroying the credence of gay people. But there are no positive words. The ideological intent of our language makes it very clear that the generation of words and meanings is, at the moment, in the hands of the enemy. And that so many gay people pretend to be straight, and call each other "butch dykes" or "screaming queens," only makes that fact the more real.

The verbal attack on men and women who do not behave as they are supposed to, reflects the ideology of masculine superiority. A man who behaves like a woman is seen as losing something, and a woman who behaves like a man is put down for threatening men's enjoyment of their privileges.

If our upbringing so often produces guilt and shame, the experience of an adult gay person is oppressive in every aspect. In their work situation, gay people face the ordeal of spending up to fifty years of their lives confronted with the antihomosexual hostility of their fellow employees.

A direct consequence of the fact that virtually all employers are highly privileged heterosexual men is that there are some fields of work which are closed to gay people, and others which they feel some compulsion to enter. A result of this control for gay women is that they are perceived as a threat in the man's world. They have none of the sexual ties of dependence to men which make most women accept men as their "superiors." They are less likely to have the bind of children, and so there is nothing to stop them showing that they are as capable as any man, and thus deflating the man's ego, and exposing the myth that only men can cope with important jobs.

We are excluded from many jobs in high places where being married is the respectable guarantee, but being homosexual apparently makes us unstable, unreliable security risks. Neither, for example, are we allowed the job of teaching children, because we are all reckoned to be compulsive, child-molesting maniacs.

There are thousands of examples of people having lost their jobs due to it becoming known that they were gay, though employers usually contrive all manner of spurious "reasons."

There occurs, on the other hand, in certain jobs such a concentration of gay people as to make an occupational ghetto. This happens, for women, in the armed forces, ambulance driving, and other uniformed occupations; and for men, in the fashion, entertainment and theatrical professions, all cases where the roles of "man" and "woman" can perhaps be underplayed or even reversed.

If you live in Scotland or Ireland; if you are under twenty-one, or over twenty-one but having sex with someone under twenty-one; if you are in the armed forces or the merchant navy; if you have sex with more than one other person at the same time —*and you are a gay male*—you are breaking the law.

The 1967 Sexual Offences Act gave a limited license to adult gay men. Common law, however, can restrict us from talking about and publicizing both male and female homosexuality by classing it as "immoral." Beyond this there is a whole series of specific minor offenses. Although "the act" is not illegal, asking someone to go to bed with you can be classed as "importuning for an immoral act," and kissing in public is classed as "public indecency."

Even if you do not get into trouble, you will find yourself hampered by the application of the law in your efforts to set up home together, to raise children, and to express your love as freely as straight people may do.

The practice of the police in "enforcing" the law makes sure that cottagers and cruisers will be zealously hunted, while queer-bashers may be apprehended, half-heartedly, after the event.

On 25 September 1969, a man walked onto Wimbledon Common. We know the common to be a popular cruising ground, and believe the man to have been one of our gay brothers. He was set upon by a group of youths from a nearby housing estate and literally battered to death with clubs and boots. Afterwards, a boy from the same estate said, "When you're hitting a queer, you can get it off him—there's nothing to be scared of from the law, 'cause you know they won't go to the law." (Sunday Times, 7/2/71)

Since that time, another man has been similarly murdered on Hampstead Heath. But murder is only the most extreme form of violence to which we are exposed, not having the effective rights of protection. Most frequently we are "rolled" for our money, or just beaten up; and this happens to butch-looking women in some districts.

One way of oppressing people and preventing their getting too angry about it is to convince them, and everyone else, that they are sick. There has hence arisen a body of psychiactric "theory" and "therapy" to deal with the "problems" and "treatment" of homosexuality.

Bearing in mind what we have so far described, it is quite understandable that gay people get depressed and paranoid; but it is also, of course, part of the scheme that gay people should retreat to psychiatrists in times of trouble.

Operating as they do on the basis of social convention and prejudice, *not* scientific truth, mainstream psychiatrists accept society's prevailing view that the male and female sex roles are "good" and "normal," and try to adjust people to them. If that fails, patients are told to "accept themselves" as "deviant." For the psychiatrist to state that homosexuality was perfectly valid and satisfying, and that the hang-up was society's inability to accept that fact, would result in the loss of a large proportion of his patients.

Psychiatric "treatment" can take the form either of mind-bending "psychotherapy," or of aversion therapy, which operates on the crude conditioning theory that if you hit a person hard enough, he'll do what you want. Another form of "therapy" is chemically induced castration, and there is a further form of "treatment" which consists of erasing part of the brain, with the intent (usually successful) of making the subject an asexual vegetable.

This "therapy" is not the source of the psychiatrists' power, however. Their social power stems from the facile and dangerous arguments by which they contrive to justify the prejudice that homosexuality is bad or unfortunate, and to mount this fundamental attack upon our right to do as we think best. In this respect, there is little difference between the psychiatrist who says "from statistics we can show that homosexuality is connected with madness," and the one who says "homosexuality is unfortunate because it is socially rejected." *The former is a dangerous idiot—he cannot see that it is society which drives gay people mad. The second is a pig because he sees this but sides consciously with the oppressors.*

That psychiatrists command such credence and such income is surprising if we remember the hysterical disagreements of theory and practice in their field, and the fact that in formulating their opinions they rarely consult gay people. In fact, so far as is possible, they avoid talking to them at all, because they know that such confrontation would wreck their theories.

The ultimate success of all forms of oppression is our self-oppression. Self-oppression is achieved when the gay person has adopted and internalized straight people's definition of what is good and bad.

Self-oppression is saying: "When you come down to it, we *are* abnormal." Or doing what you most need and want to do, but with a sense of shame and loathing, or in a state of disassociation, pretending it isn't happening; cruising or cottaging, not because you enjoy it, but because you're afraid of anything less anonymous. Self-oppression is saying "I accept what I am," and meaning "I accept that what I am is second-best and rather pathetic." Self-oppression is any other kind of apology: "We've been living together for ten years and all our married friends know about us and think we're just the same as them." Why? You're not.

Self-oppression is the dolly lesbian who says, "I can't stand those butch types who look like truck drivers"; the virile gay man who shakes his head at the thought of "those pathetic queens." This is self-oppression because it's just another way of saying: "I'm a nice normal gay, just like an attractive heterosexual."

The ultimate in self-oppression is to avoid confronting straight society, and thereby provoking further hostility: *Self-oppression is saying, and believing: "I am not oppressed."*

Why We're Oppressed

Gay people are oppressed. As we've just shown, we face the prejudice, hostility and violence of straight society, and the opportunities open to us in work and leisure are restricted, compared with those open to straight people. Shouldn't we demand reforms that will give us tolerance and equality? Certainly we should—in a liberal-democratic society, legal equality and protection from attack are the very least we should ask for. They are our civil rights.

But gay liberation does not just mean reforms. It means a revolutionary change in our whole society. Is this really necessary? Isn't it hard enough for us to win reforms within present society, and how will we engage the support of straight people if we get ourselves branded as revolutionaries?

Reforms may make things better for a while: changes in the law can make straight people a little less hostile, a little more tolerant, but reform cannot change the deep-down attitude of straight people that homosexuality is at best inferior to their own way of life, at worst a sickening perversion. It will take more than reforms to change this attitude, because it is rooted in our society's most basic institution—the Patriarchal Family.

We've all been brought up to believe that the family is the source of our happiness and comfort. But look at the family more closely. Within the small family unit, in which the dominant man and submissive woman bring up their children in their own image, all our attitudes towards sexuality are learned at a very early age. Almost before we can talk, certainly before we can think for ourselves, we are taught that there are certain attributes that are "feminine" and others that are "masculine," and that they are God-given and unchangeable. Beliefs learned so young are very hard to change; but in fact these are false beliefs. What we are taught about the differences between man and woman is propaganda, not truth.

The truth is that there are no proven systematic differences between male and female, apart from the obvious biological ones. Male and female genitals and reproductive systems are different, and so are certain other physical characteristics, but all differences of temperament, aptitudes and so on are the result of upbringing and social pressures. They are not inborn.

Human beings could be much more various than our constricted patterns of "masculine" and "feminine" permit—we should be free to develop with greater individuality. But as things are at present, there are only these two stereotyped roles into which everyone is supposed to fit, and most people—including gay people—are apt to be alarmed when they hear these stereotypes or gender roles attacked, fearing that children "won't know how to grow up if they have no one to identify with," or that "everyone will be the same," i.e., that there will either be utter chaos or total conformity. There would in fact be a greater variety of models and more freedom for experimentation, but there is no reason to suppose this would lead to chaos.

By our very existence as gay people we challenge these roles. It can easily be seen that homosexuals don't fit into the stereotypes of masculine and feminine, and this is one of the main reasons we become the object of suspicion, since everyone is taught that these, and only these, two roles are appropriate.

Our entire society is built around the patriarchal family and its enshrinement of these masculine and feminine roles. Religion, popular morality, art, literature and sport all reinforce these stereotypes. In other words, this society is a *sexist* society, in which one's biological sex determines almost all of what one does and how one does it; a situation in which men are privileged, and women are mere adjuncts of men and objects for their use, both sexually and otherwise. . . .

But why can't we just change the way in which children are brought up without attempting to transform the whole fabric of society?

Because sexism is not just an accident—*it is an essential part of our present society*, and cannot be changed without the whole society changing with it. In the first place, our society is dominated at every level by men who have an interest in preserving the status quo; secondly, the present system of work and production depends on the existence of the patriarchal family. Conservative sociologists have pointed out that the small family unit of two parents and their children is essential in our contemporary advanced industrial family, where work is minutely subdivided and highly regulated—in other words, very boring for the majority. A man would not work at the assembly line if he had no wife and family to support; he would not give himself fully to his work without the supportive and reassuring little group ready to follow him about and gear itself to his needs, to put up with his ill temper when he is frustrated or put down by the boss at work.

Were it not also for the captive wife, educated by advertising and everything she reads into believing that she needs ever more new goodies for the home, for her own beautification and for the children's well-being, our economic system could not function properly, depending as it does on people buying far more manufactured goods than they need. The housewife, obsessed with the ownership of as many material goods as possible, is the agent of this high level of spending. None of these goods will ever satisfy her, since there is always something better to be had, and the surplus of these pseudo "necessities" goes hand in hand with the absence of genuinely necessary goods and services, such as adequate housing and schools.

The ethic and ideology of our culture has been conveniently summed up by the enemy. Here is a quotation, intended quite seriously, from an American psychiatric primer. The author, Dr. Fred Brown, states:

Our values in Western civilization are founded upon the sanctity of the family, the right to property, and the worthwhileness of "getting ahead." The family can be established only through heterosexual intercourse, and this gives the woman a high value. Property acquisition and worldly success are viewed as distinctly masculine aims. The individual who is outwardly masculine but appears to fall into the feminine class by reason . . . of his preference for other men denies these values of our civilization. In denying them he belittles those goals which carry weight and much emotional coloring in our society and thereby earns the hostility of those to whom these values are of great importance.

We agree with his description of our society and its values—but we reach a different conclusion. We gay men and gay women *do* deny these values of our civilization. We believe that the society Dr. Brown describes is an evil society. We believe that work in an advanced industrial society could be organized on more humane lines, with each job more varied and more pleasurable, and that the way society is at present organized operates in the interests of a small ruling group of straight men who claim most of the status and money, and not in the interests of the people as a whole. We also believe that our economic resources could be used in a much more valuable and constructive way than they are at the moment—but that will not happen until the present pattern of male dominance in our society changes too.

That is why any reforms we might painfully exact from our rulers would only be fragile and vulnerable; that is why we, along with the women's movement, must fight for something more than reform. We must aim at the abolition of the family, so that the sexist, male-supremacist system can no longer be nurtured there.

We Can Do It

Yet although this struggle will be hard, and our victories not easily won, we are not in fact being idealistic to aim at abolishing the family and the cultural distinctions between men and women. True, these have been with us throughout history, yet humanity is at least in a position where we can progress beyond this. . . .

But linked with this struggle to change society there is an important aspect of gay liberation that we can begin to build here and now—a *new*, *liberated lifestyle* which will anticipate, as far as possible, the free society of the future.

Gay shows the way. In some ways we are already more advanced than straight people. We are already outside the family and we have already, in part at least, rejected the "masculine" or "feminine" roles society has designed for us. In a society dominated by the sexist culture it is very difficult, if not impossible, for heterosexual men and women to escape their rigid gender-role structuring and the roles of oppressor and oppressed. But gay men don't need to oppress women in order to fulfill their own psychosexual needs, and gay women don't have to relate sexually to the male oppressor, so that at this moment in time, the freest and most equal relationships are most likely to be between homosexuals.

But because the sexist culture has oppressed us and distorted *our* lives too, this is not always achieved. In our mistaken, placating efforts to be accepted and tolerated, we've too often submitted to the pressures to conform to the straitjacket of society's rules and hang-ups about sex . . .

It is especially important for gay people to stop copying straight—we are the ones who have the best opportunities to create a new lifestyle and if we don't, no one else will. Also, we need one another more than straight people need one another, because we are equals suffering under an insidious oppression from a society too primitive to come to terms with the freedom we represent. Singly, or isolated in couples, we are weak—the way society wants us to be. Society cannot put us down so easily if we fuse together. *We have to get together, understand one another, live together.* Two ways we can do this are by developing consciousness-raising groups and by gay communes.

Our gay communes and collectives must not be mere convenient living arrangements—or worse, just extensions of the gay ghetto. They must be a focus of consciousness-raising (i.e., raising or increasing our awareness of our real oppression) and of gay liberation activity, a new focal point for members of the gay community. It won't be easy, because this society is hostile to communal living. And besides the practical hang-ups of finding money and a place large enough for a collective to live, there are our own personal hang-ups: we have to change our attitudes to our personal property, to our lovers, to our day-to-day priorities in work and leisure, even to our need for privacy.

But victory will come. If we're convinced of the importance of the new lifestyle, we can be strong and we can win through....

step may

high school days

"This day is dedicated to the one hundred thirty-five Elk Grove High School kids who will one day fight for the right to love a member of the same sex."

Wednesday: six members of Gay Liberation—one gay woman, four gay men, and Susan, the Polymorphous Perverse—travel to a white middle-class suburban high school to talk to a succession of sociology classes.

The six of us sit facing the class; the kids sit quietly, listening. What's going on inside their heads? Do they hate us, are they afraid of us? Do they view us as a curiosity? It occurs to me that the most freaked-out person in the room may be one of the gay high school kids in his closet, struggling to control his emotions, not to let it show. His face is calm, he sits quietly, while his guts are ripping apart, his mind in turmoil.

We each give a short rap, then open it up to discussion. A girl asks us why we set ourselves apart from straight society, why we alienate ourselves. I tell her that the straight world sets us apart, not we ourselves. I tell her we're alienated because we don't marry members of the opposite sex, settle in Elk Grove Village, have kids.

Another student asks why, if God wanted homosexuality, did he first create a heterosexual couple? Someone else answers, while I frame my own, silent answer in my mind. It doesn't matter what it says in the Bible; it's fantasy, it's made up. I don't care what God wanted. It's what I want that matters. But I don't say that —wouldn't want them to think all homosexuals are atheists.

Richard talks about his parents. "My parents know I'm gay. Their reactions are rather typical. My father tells me to go see a psychiatrist. My mother thinks I've made a bad decision." The kids crack up. It's great to hear them laugh. It says to us that they know that nobody *decides* to be gay: that we feel it in our guts, the same as straight people.

Another girl speaks up. (We've received five or six responses from girls. Not a single one from a guy. Why? Are the guys really that uptight, that insecure about their sexuality?) She asks, what determines whether a person becomes a heterosexual or a homosexual? Shelly answers that a gay man usually has a traumatic experience in his background. A woman's gayness is determined more by social context. I disagree. I don't think science has anything to say about sexuality. Neither social science, physical science, nor biological science. I say so. There's disagreement on the panel. Gay Liberation has no correct line.

A couple of guys finally speak up. That's an improvement.

There's humor, honesty, exchange of ideas. Kids asking questions that would shock their parents. Have you ever slept with a member of the opposite sex? Do you want to have sex with every member of the same sex that you see?

(We've just learned that the local press has been alerted to our presence, possibly by an alarmed parent. A reporter is on her way. We'll drive off this afternoon, leaving the sociology team and the principal to deal with the coming storm. We won't even be aware of whatever goes on after we depart . . . hit and run: gay guerrillas.)

Toward the end of each period I declare that there are three or four or five gay kids in the room besides ourselves. My friends tell me after second period that I'm putting the gay kids uptight, that they must think for one terrified second that I've spotted them, will point them out. So I change my rap. "According to the Kinsey Report, 5 percent of the population is gay. We can therefore expect that 5 percent of the kids in this class are gay, blah, blah . . ." I tell the gay kids, whoever they may be, that they should memorize the telephone number written on the board (they won't incriminate themselves by copying it down) and call if they want to talk about it. I wonder what I would have done if I'd been a high school senior and had suddenly been presented with a number I could call to talk to a fellow homosexual for the first time. I wonder if I would have called.

(In fact, it was in high school that I first became aware that I was gay. A friend asked me what homosexual meant. I looked it up in the dictionary and was mind-blown to find that the definition described an aspect of me. The story of my gay birth in front of an unabridged dictionary is unique. The rest of the Toms River High School story is the same as the Elk Grove High School story. I'm telling the gay kids a history that they're living, that they know, but probably haven't heard told before.)

"I couldn't tell any of my friends that I was gay. I was ashamed. I thought I was perverted, a freak. I couldn't sit around with the other kids when they were carrying on about their current crushes [that had to be deferred until now, when at twenty-two I babble on incessantly about the guy I like]. I couldn't go out on dates with guys, didn't want to go to parties or dances with girls. The worst part is having to internalize it all. You pack in the unspent energy, the untold thoughts, the unrealized longings, the unreleased emotions, pack 'em in, pack 'em in, until you think you're going to blow apart. But you never do. Just painful day after tormented day after anguished day."

As I say this I know it sounds awfully maudlin—yet I must, so that no one will get the idea that it isn't hell. Because it is. People should know that. I feel a great love and concern for the gay kids in the class, a great empathy for their suffering. I wonder if any of them will call.

Now it's fifth period and the room is packed. Kids on the floor, against the walls, sharing seats. The atmosphere is electric, everyone has a sense that something special is happening. We hardly have a chance to start our short presentations when hands start waving. Someone tells us she's had a puritanical upbringing. "Shouldn't some temptations be resisted? Should moral values be generated from within a person or should they come from an outside source?" I ask her, what outside source —Church? State? Yes, the Church is what she had in mind. I reply that religion has nothing to tell me, that it's a bunch of myths. I'm surprised when there's a burst of applause. We talk about morality, about happiness, about hurting people. "In terms of hurting people," I say, "the Church is the most immoral institution in the world." Oh brother, now I've done it. A gay atheist. Does anyone suspect that I'm a communist? Yet before I know it, I'm doing it again. I'm attacking the family, marriage. "A child should not be subject to the domination and absolute dictates of the two people who happen to be his biological parents. Children should be raised communally by all adults—men, women, gays, straights." There's no response to this one. The kids are hearing it for the first time. I only heard it myself for the first time a few weeks ago. I had to think about it. Now they'll think about it. I'm glad I said it.

Someone asks me if my parents know. Not yet. It wasn't too hard for me to come out, because my parents are in New Jersey, a good safe distance away. But you're going to see some real courage when gay high school kids start coming out, telling their friends, being up-front, organizing. Two guys'll go to the prom together. Their four parents will look down from the balcony and agree that Jimmy and Tommy make a cute couple. We'll celebrate the day that High School Gay Liberation gets rolling at home. They're gonna start dating. A girl's gonna call up a girl she likes and ask her if she wants to go to the movies. "If you don't wanna go," she'll tell her, "just say no." Gay kids'll dance together wherever straight kids dance. Two guys'll walk down the hall holding hands. They'll protest when they're discriminated against, they're not gonna take that shit anymore. And they'll be happy. That's right, folks. Gay high school students will be happy. I hope the first High School Gay Liberation group is at Elk Grove. Young Gay Pioneers. I'll be proud of them.

"I've heard about suburban high school sociology. One day an ex-convict comes in. He tells how he's seen the error of his ways. He's reformed and things are much better than they were (aren't they?). Then a dope addict who's kicked the habit. A prostitute who's gotten a 'decent' job. So here's your homosexual. Only he's not reforming. Nothing to reform. Only to liberate. Things are gonna be so much better."

 **dear abby**
odd couple

About four months ago, the house across the street was sold to a "father and son"—or so we thought. We later learned it was an older man about fifty and a young fellow about twenty-four.

This was a respectable neighborhood before this "odd couple" moved in. They have all sorts of strange-looking company. Men who look like women, and women who look like men; blacks, whites, Indians. Yesterday I even saw two nuns go in there.

They must be running some sort of business, or a club. There are motorcycles, expensive sports cars, and even bicycles parked in front and on the lawn. They keep their shades drawn so you can't see what's going on inside but they must be up to no good, or why the secrecy?

We called the police department and they asked if we wanted to press charges. They said unless the neighbors were breaking some law there was nothing they could do.
These weirdos are wrecking our property values! How can we improve the quality of the respectable neighborhood?

Up in Arms

Dear Up:
You could move.

gore vidal

bisexual politics

I was twenty-one when I wrote *The City and the Pillar*. Although I had already published two novels, *Williwaw* and *In a Yellow Mood,* my talent was not precocious. I knew how to do a few things well, and I did them all in *Williwaw*. By the time I came to write *The City and the Pillar,* I was bored with playing it safe. I wanted to take risks, to try something no American had done before. I decided to examine the homosexual underworld (which I knew rather less well than I pretended), and in the process show the "naturalness" of homosexual rela-tions, as well as making the point that there is of course no such thing as a homosexual. Despite current usage, the word is an adjec-tive describing a sexual action, not a noun describing a recognizable type. All human beings are bisexual. Conditioning, oppor-tunity and habit account finally (and mys-teriously) for sexual preference, and ho-mosexualists are quite as difficult to gen-eralize about as heterosexualists. They range from the transvestite who believes himself to be Bette Davis to the perfectly ordinary citizen who regards boys with the same uncomplicated lust with which his brother regards girls.

When legal and social pressures against homosexuality are particularly severe, homosexualists can become neurotic, in much the same way Jews and Negroes do in a hostile environment. Yet a man who enjoys sensual relations with his own sex is not, by definition, neurotic. In any event, categorizing is impossible. Particularly when one considers that most homosexualists marry and become fathers, which makes them, technically, bisexual, a condition whose existence is firmly denied by at least one school of psychiatry on the odd ground that a man *must* be one thing or the other, which is demonstrably untrue. Admittedly, no two things are equal, and so a man is bound to prefer one specific to another, but that does not mean that under the right stimulus, and at another time, he might not accommodate himself to both. It is interesting to note that the current slang word for someone both sophisticated and enviable is "swinger." And what is a swinger? One who swings both ways, who is able to take pleasure where he finds it, with either sex.

In 1946, when I wrote *The City and the Pillar,* it was a part of American folklore that homosexuality was a form of mental disease, confined for the most part to interior decorators and ballet dancers. Knowing this to be untrue, I set out to shatter the stereotype by taking as my protagonist a completely ordinary boy of the middle class and through his eyes observe the various strata of the underworld. This was a considerable act of imagination. I came from a political family. Jim Willard and I shared the same geography, but little else. Also, in the interest of verisimilitude I decided to tell the story in a flat gray prose reminiscent of one of James T. Farrell's social documents. There was to be nothing fancy in the writing. I wanted the prose plain and hard and, if I may say so, I succeeded.

Contemplating the American scene in the 1940s, Mr. Stephen Spender deplored the machinery of literary success, remarking sternly that "One has only to follow the whizzing comet of . . . Gore Vidal to see how quickly and effectively this transforming, diluting, disintegrating machinery can work." He then characterized *The City and the Pillar* as a work of sexual confession, quite plainly autobiography at its most artless. Transformed, diluted, disintegrated as I was, I found this description flattering. Mr. Spender had paid me a considerable compliment, for though I am the least autobiographical of novelists, apparently I had drawn the character of the athlete Jim Willard so convincingly that to this day aging pederasts are firmly convinced that

I was once a male prostitute, with an excellent backhand at tennis. The truth, alas, is quite another matter.

When the book was published in 1948, it was received with shock and disbelief. How could that young war novelist (last observed in the pages of *Life* magazine posed like Jack London against a ship) turn into this? The *New York Times* refused to take advertising for the book, and most of the reviews were hostile. The press lectured me firmly on the delights of heterosexual love, while chiding the publishers for distributing such a lurid "memoir." Nevertheless, the book was a best seller, not only in the United States but in Europe, where it was taken seriously by critics, not all engaged. André Gide presented me with a copy of *Corydon*, as one prophet to another. E. M. Forster invited me to Cambridge and shyly confessed that he had written a somewhat similar book which he had never published, not wanting to embarrass family and friends. "Quite bold, actually," he said. In what way, I asked. Apparently there was a scene of two boys in bed. "And what," I asked, intrigued, "do they do?" Mr. Forster smiled. "They . . . *talk*," he said, with some satisfaction. Later that year, in a statistical report, Dr. Kinsey revealed what American men are actually up to, and I was somewhat exonerated for my candor. I even received a nice letter from the good doctor, complimenting me on "your work in the field."

The world has changed a good deal since 1948. Sexual candor is now not only common, but obligatory. Outright pornography is published openly and I doubt if it does much harm. After all, Americans like how-to-do books. But, most significant, young people today are in many ways more relaxed about sexual matters than we were in the 1940s. They have discovered that choice of sexual partner is a matter of taste, not of divine or even "natural" law. Also, I suspect that the psychological basis to most sex is not so much physical satisfaction as it is a will to power. This strikes me as implicit in *The City and the Pillar,* though I was perfectly unaware of it at the time. When a young man rejects the advances of another young man, his motive, often as not, is a fear of losing autonomy, of being used as a thing by the other, conquered instead of conquering. . . .

In its slow way, our society is beginning to shed many of its superstitions about the sexual act. The idea that there is no such thing as "normality" is at last penetrating the tribal consciousness, although the religiously inclined still regard nonprocreative sex as "unnatural," while the statistically inclined regard as "normal" only what the

majority does. Confident that most sexual acts are heterosexual, the consensus maintains that heterosexuality, as the preferred form of erotic expression, must be ''right.'' However, following that line of reasoning to its logical conclusion, one would have to recognize that the most frequently performed sexual act is neither hetero- nor homosexual but onanistic, and surely, even in a total democracy, masturbation would not be declared the perfect norm from which all else is deviation. In any case, sex of any sort is neither right nor wrong. It is.

The Kissing Booth at Gay Happening/Los Angeles, Summer 1971

gary alinder

my gay soul

A few weeks ago a gay brother and I interviewed a lawyer who is
a kind of Charles Garry for the gay community in San Francisco.
I asked him if he is gay. He said, "If you're trying to get me to say
I'm queer, I won't do it. What I do in bed is nobody's business."

I wanted to scream, "Honey, I don't care what you do in bed,
I just asked if you are gay."

A few days later I was rapping with some women who are heavy
into Women's Liberation. "You zero in on sex; you always zero in
on sex," they said. I've been told the same thing by liberal homosexuals and straights alike: "What you do in bed is your business,
do your thing." They are saying that gay means SEX, nothing but sex.

Well, I'm tired to the bone of being told what I am. I am gay.
Yes, yes, my cock, my mouth and my asshole are gay. So are my
fingernails, my big toe, my nose and my brain. I am not gay because
of where I put my cock or who I sleep with. I am gay because
everything about me is gay, because I am part of a gay community.

I was gay long before I admitted my homosexuality to myself, long before I had sex, long before I knew what sex was.

When I was ten, I played paper dolls with the girls and dug it; when I had to, I played baseball with the guys and didn't dig it.

When I was thirteen a gang of four or five guys tormented me, all through junior high school. They called me a cocksucker. I didn't know what it meant, but I knew it was the worst thing a guy could call another guy. They called me "Mrs. Alinder." They probably had homosexual fantasies and wanted to relate to me physically and the only way they could do it was to provoke me to fight them. But I didn't. I was scared shitless. There were five of them, and I was alone.

I grew up on a farm in southern Minnesota, where you proved your masculinity in competitive athletics. I had too much self-doubt to be any good. In high school I earned a bit of respect through journalism, theater and art. But I was never the man I was supposed to be, although I did drive a tractor, plow the fields, toss bales of hay into the hay loft and join the Future Farmers of America.

I went to a small liberal arts college near my home for two years. It was a super-straight middle-class parochial place, everything based on a social pecking order of fraternities and sororities. Even the lowest fraternity, a bunch of creeps, didn't want me. Did I have B.O.? Bad breath? No. I was hipper and in some ways more together than they. But I couldn't censor myself enough. My gay self was showing through. And my gay self was me. And every response I got from the world told me that my gay self was despicable. So I censored myself more, built higher and thicker walls around my soul and retreated deeper into my closet.

I had friends, other guys at the bottom. I was afraid to be seen on campus with them. I thought I would slip even lower. We were all gay, but that could never be talked about, never be acted out. We were the outcasts, but we were not together.

Two years later a good friend came out. Finally I admitted that I was gay too. We had been friends since we were seven years old. But it was not until we were twenty-two and twenty-three that we could deal with what brought us together. Since then, although we live far apart, I've felt very close to that friend. We've been through a lot.

What separates me from the straight boy is not just the things we do in bed, but what our lives have been. When I meet an upfront gay brother, I make a connection. I already know a lot about him.

I need to be together with other gay men. We have not been together—we've not had enough self-respect for that. Isolated sex, from one partner to the next. Enough of that. That's where we've been; let's go somewhere else. Let's go where we value each other as more than just a hunk of meat. We need to recognize one another wherever we are, start talking to each other. We need to say "Hi, brother" when we see each other on the street. We need consciousness-raising groups and communes.

Our gay souls have nearly been stomped to death in that desert called America. If we are to bloom, we can only do it together.

I need you, brother, because brother, you are all I have.

huey newton

a letter from huey

During the past few years, strong movements have developed among women and homosexuals seeking their liberation. There has been some uncertainty about how to relate to these movements. Whatever your personal opinion and your insecurities about homosexuality and the various liberation movements among homosexuals and women (and I speak of homosexuals and women as oppressed groups), we should try to unite with them in revolutionary fashion.

I say "whatever your insecurities are" because, as we very well know, sometimes our first instinct is to want to hit a homosexual in the mouth and to want a woman to be quiet. We want to hit the homosexual in the mouth as soon as we see him because we're afraid we might be homosexual, and we want to hit the woman or shut her up because we're afraid she might castrate us to take the nuts we may not have to start with.

We must gain security in ourselves and therefore have respect and feelings for all oppressed people. We must not use the racist-type attitudes the white racists use against people because they are black and poor. Many times the poorest white person is the most racist because he's afraid he might lose something or discover something that he doesn't have. You're some kind of threat to him. This kind of psychology is in operation when we view oppressed people and we're angry with them because of their particular kind of behavior or their particular kind of deviation from the established norm.

Remember, we haven't established a revolutionary value system; we're only in the process of establishing it. I don't remember us ever constituting any value that said that a revolutionary must say offensive things toward homosexuals or that a revolutionary must make sure women don't speak out about their own particular kind of oppression.

Matter of fact, it's just the opposite: we say that we recognize the woman's right to be free. We haven't said much about the homosexual at all and we must relate to the homosexual movement because it is a real movement. And I know through reading and through my life experience, my observation, that homosexuals are not given freedom and liberty by anyone in this society. Maybe they might be the most oppressed people in the society.

What made them homosexuals? Perhaps it's a whole phenomenon that I don't understand entirely. Some people say that it's the decadence of capitalism—I don't know whether this is the case, I rather doubt it. But whatever the case is, we know that homosexuality is a fact, that it exists, that we must understand it in its purest form; that is, a person should have the freedom to use his body whatever way he wants to.

That's not endorsing things in homosexuality that we wouldn't view as revolutionary. But there is nothing to say that a homosexual cannot also be a revolutionary. And maybe I'm now injecting some of my prejudice by saying "even a homosexual can be a revolutionary." Quite the contrary; maybe a homosexual could be the most revolutionary.

When we have revolutionary conferences, rallies and demonstrations, there should be full participation of the Gay Liberation Movement and the Women's Liberation Movement. Some groups might be more revolutionary than others. We shouldn't use the actions of a few to say that they're all reactionary or counterrevolutionary, because they're not.

We should deal with factions just as we deal with any other group or party that claims to be revolutionary. We should try to judge somehow whether they're operating sincerely in a revolutionary fashion from a really oppressed situation (and we'll grant that if they're women they're probably oppressed). If they do things that are unrevolutionary or counterrevolutionary, then criticize that action. If we feel that the group in spirit means to be revolutionary in practice but they make mistakes in interpretation of the revolutionary philosophy or they don't understand the dialectics of the social forces in operation, we should criticize that, and not criticize them because they are women trying to be free. And the same is true for homosexuals.

We should never say a whole movement is dishonest when in fact they are trying to be honest; they're just making honest mistakes. Friends are allowed to make mistakes. The enemy is not allowed to make mistakes because his whole existence is a mistake and we suffer from it. But the Women's Liberation Front and Gay Liberation Front are our friends, they are our potential allies and we need as many allies as possible.

We should be willing to discuss the insecurities that many people have about homosexuality. When I say "insecurities" I mean the fear that there is some kind of threat to our manhood. I can understand this fear. Because of the long conditioning process that builds insecurity in the American male, homosexuality might produce certain hangups in us. I have hangups myself about male homosexuality where on the other hand I have no hangups about female homosexuality. I think it's probably because male homosexuals may be a threat to me, and the females aren't. It's just another erotic sexual thing.

We should be careful about using terms which might turn our friends off. The terms "faggot" and "punk" should be deleted from our vocabulary and especially we should not attach names normally designed for homosexuals to men who are enemies of the people, such as Nixon or Mitchell. Homosexuals are not enemies of the people.

We should try to form a working coalition with the Gay Liberation and Women's Liberation groups. We must always handle social forces in an appropriate manner and

this is really a significant part of the population—both women and the growing number of homosexuals that we have to deal with.

ALL POWER TO THE PEOPLE!

Huey P. Newton
Supreme Commander,
Black Panther Party

Woodcut by Perry Brass

konstantin berlandt

bring the
beautiful boys home

BEAUTIFUL GIs, soft naked shoulders sweating in the Vietnamese sun
looking over their naked shoulders for the bullet from the crackling leaf in the jungles
looking over their naked shoulders for CID man who's gonna bust them for dope
   who's gonna bust them for love, who's gonna dress them in pink tennis shoes,
   pin their heads down over their cocks between their legs,
   throw them out dishonorably, send them to jail, send them to the front lines.

Gonna have those beautiful shoulders sliced with bayonets,
   sliced up like shoulder roasts, blood pouring from the crevices
      blood spattered across the blue sky
         across the sparkling sun
       that glares in the camera lens
        a red explosion across your color TV

I was just watching a beautiful boy, beautiful naked shoulders

    I wanted to touch and kiss him
          I love him:

* This poem was part of a leaflet for the October 1969 Moratorium distributed by Gay Liberation in San Francisco and Berkeley.

My boyfriend from high school P.E.
  My boyfriend from commuter-cycle rides to college from El Cerrito
   My boyfriend from the newspaper
    My boyfriend from sociology class
     My boyfriend high up on the balcony of the Student Union
      My boyfriend swimming naked in Yosemite's backcountry Washburn Lake

          My boyfriend in bed with me
              kissing my cock
I snapped you on the butt with my towel
  I held you tight from the back of your motorcycle
    I put my hand on your shoulder before we said good night after our double-date
     I held your hand on the walk to your house to study with you
      I held your feet as you slid into the sky

Into the sea,
        I swam under you, I swam around you
        I stroked your naked liquid body in the icy water
Soaped your body in the shower
and rubbed against it
            kissing your cock

Let me lick up the blood
  of my gay brother
Wrap up his remains—
   his foot, his eyeball—in a towel dripping with blood
   and put them back on my bed for me to play with
I'll lick my sheets so my mother doesn't know I had company on the rag
    Soak the sheets in cold water
      Spread them out on the line in the sun.

Well, you can do your thing. Just stay away from me.
I want to go on hating and killing, hating and killing.
Hi there, Gook. Let me cut your beautiful body up limb by limb
Let me cut off your cock and put it in my pocket as a trophy-souvenir

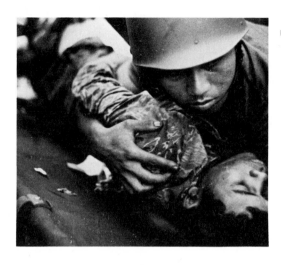

Dying soldier/South Vietnam

Don't touch me, queer!
I dig chicks, Vietnamese whores.
I didn't know you were queer, George
you know it's against regulations.
   Don't kiss me now, friend,
    while the sergeant is watching.

Beautiful Vietnamese man
Let's suck and fuck
Let's not kill each other any more
I love you brother
You're my buddy
We're gonna die tomorrow
I want to hold your cock and
   make it feel good tonight
I want to put my cock in your body
   and feel together with you
         tonight

italian gay libletter

We are a minority and therefore have revolutionary potential. But it is evident that this potential will burst forth only if brought into the light of day; it won't do to keep it buried.

What are we asking of you? To come out!

What do we propose? A gay activism.

What do we want? To reject integration into the society.

—Not to tolerate intolerance.

This piece is translated from Italy's first gay liberation newspaper, *Fuori* ("Come Out"). It started publishing in Torino, Italy, in the spring of 1972 and is edited by Torino's active gay liberation organization.—The editors

—Not to tolerate tolerance.

—To live our homosexuality fully, not giving a damn for the niceties of bourgeois society or the narrowmindedness of the left.

—To have the right to do whatever we want with our own bodies.

—To tear down the bourgeois myth of the sacrilegiousness of the asshole, a myth especially developed among the proletariat.

—To abolish such terms as "fag" and "queer," sissy and fairy.

—To eliminate the classifications and distinctions passive and active, above and below, cylinder and piston.

—Not to have to produce goods (children) or be consumers (wives).

154

To make revolution you have to have one or more antagonists; if they don't exist, you have to create them. Here is a list which can be added to easily:

MOTHER: Cries when she learns we're homosexual.

FATHER: Wants to disown us.

BROTHERS AND SISTERS: Are afraid of catching it.

AUNTS: Believe themselves to be the direct cause by means of alternating hereditary cycles.

HUMOR: We are one of its most sparkling subjects.

HOMOSEXUALS: Those who camouflage themselves and don't come out.

HETEROSEXUALS: Those who believe themselves to be the sexual norm.

SEX: In its least liberated, i.e., bars, urinals, saunas, pools, parks.

TOLERANT SOCIETY: Accuses the other half of intolerance and then says we are sick.

PSYCHIATRY: Says we are "curable" and therefore sick.

MARX: Ignores the question of sex.

MARXISTS: Say homosexuality is a decadent bourgeois disease.

THE PROLETARIAT: Creators of the myth of the masculine, virile man. In the style of Marlon Brando in *On the Waterfront*.

MARXISM-LENINISM: Ignores us because Marx ignored us.

HITLER: Eliminated us in concentration camps.

MAO: Eliminated ten thousand of us in the Night of the Long Knives. (But this might be a capitalist tale.)

CASTRO: Castrates us.

THE GREATS: Shakespeare, Michelangelo, Leonardo, Caesar, Alexander, etc., etc., whom we present with pride as magnificent examples: They too! They too!

155

louis landerson

france's own gay liberation

Over the last few years, along with some of the more obnoxious aspects of American culture, several important political ideas have been spreading to France, expanding the realm of traditional politics to what is now called "existential problems." Gay liberation, like the women's movement, is among those imported political conceptions.

The FHAR (Front Homosexuel d'Action Révolutionnaire), main organ of gay liberation in Paris, was formed in March 1971 after a group of lesbians and faggots disrupted one of those humdrum radio discussions which just happened to be entitled "Homosexuality, This Painful Problem." A year and a half before, in September 1970, a group of lesbians had contacted the MLF (French Women's Liberation Movement), wanting to form a revolutionary lesbian movement. Over a year later they were joined by a small group of faggots and it was this mixed group which carried out the action that generated the FHAR.

Since that time FHAR people have participated in May Day celebrations, Mother's Day celebrations, picnics at the Tuileries, a demonstration against psychiatrists in San Remo, Italy—pretty much the same kinds of things we've been doing here. There have also been rap groups, consciousness-raising groups, guerrilla theatre, and seminars.

The greatest impetus for growth to the FHAR was the April 1971 issue of *Tout,* which was devoted almost entirely to gay liberation. *Tout* is a straight, leftist-student-underground newspaper whose director is Jean-Paul Sartre. Shortly after the FHAR was formed, one of the staff members of *Tout,* who is gay, became involved in gay liberation. He suggested that the FHAR people do some writing. Articles began appearing and the people at *Tout* were eventually persuaded to let the queers speak. And speak they did.

(Before getting to the gay articles in this, the twelfth, issue of *Tout,* the reader had to plow through a statement of the editors —who were mostly straight *and* mostly male. Unfortunately, this statement reduced everything to an "everyone has the right to do his own thing" kind of position. What was important about the statement was that it was the first discussion on the political implications of personal/sexual relations —basically talking about a new awareness coming out of the women's movement.)

The FHAR articles reflect the lucidity of the French mind, with lots of Marxist and anarchist rhetoric thrown in, and a touch of Marcuse. The main thrust of the articles is anti-capitalist and anti-imperialist, with

a sharp critique of the puritan sexuality of French culture. In a statement of purpose, the FHAR claims:

We are against homosexuality as we are against heterosexuality; these are words which take reality only in a socially determined context. It is necessary to destroy this social context so the words will no longer have any meaning. The same goes for relations between men and women, for the family and for the notion of power: we are against whoever presumes to seize power, whatever the ideology with which he identifies himself. Power is not for the taking; it is the notion of power that is to be destroyed.

They also criticize the idealization of virility, gender-programming, and bourgeois psychiatry. But their biggest problem is with the left.

In a country where the orthodox conception of class struggle is still very strong, it is difficult for the voice of sexual politics to make itself heard. According to many Marxists (the Cuban National Congress on Education and Culture, for example), there is no material basis for the oppression of homosexuals. So, accepting the terms dictated by orthodox Marxism, the FHAR articles argue against the kind of straight male mentality which refuses to recognize the validity of psychological oppression. They criticize the validity of psychological oppression. They criticize the male supremacy and repressed sexuality of straight revolutionaries and attack the sexual revolution as a sexist bourgeois plot. Their position is perhaps best summed up in the following:

The struggle for gay liberation is not a marginal combat. Revolutionary homosexuals refuse the puritanical terrorism of certain militants who use as a mask the pretext of the necessity for the struggle of the masses. It is true that in France there exists only a weak minority of avowed homosexuals, and this is because in certain sectors of the bourgeoisie, particularly among artists and intellectuals, homosexuality is tolerated or even asserted, and doesn't tarnish one's social reputation. But there exist as well, and especially amongst the masses, hundreds of thousands of homosexuals who are repressed and who are very down on themselves because of the burden that bourgeois moral ideology has imposed upon them. The fact that they have not yet been united by a collective consciousness is not a good enough reason to pretend that the notion of the "masses" is not applicable to them.

Homosexual revolutionaries know that homosexuality does not originate in the socio-economic structures of bourgeois capitalism and consequently that the first will not disappear with the destruction of the second.

(Ask our Cuban friends about *that*!)

After the publication of these articles, there was a Storm of Controversy, as it were. Irate citizens wrote in letters of disgust, disappointment, etc.; the government banned the newspaper from newsstands. But there were also a lot of gay people who spoke out for the first time in their lives.

Before *l'affaire Tout*, the FHAR had about thirty people; after, membership rose to seven hundred in Paris, and groups started forming all over the country. Along with success came hassles, as gay revolutionaries were faced with the problem of integrating seven hundred people of varying race, age, sex, and class into a unified revolutionary movement. It didn't work.

Most of what has come out of Paris since April 1971 talks about all the difficulties the FHAR is unable to resolve. One article, in the January 1972 *Nouvel Observateur* (the most widely distributed leftist weekly in France), talked about how chaotic the FHAR meetings are and how difficult it is to carry out any kind of political action. Some revolutionaries are breaking ranks because the group doesn't come up to Marxist-Leninist-Maoist standards. I have been writing to one member of FHAR; in his last letter he was discouraged, saying we can speak of the FHAR as a mass movement only in the past.

But the problems of FHAR—in-group tensions, elitism, alienation of newcomers, total lack of concensus—are not after all so very different from the problems we once had in the Gay Liberation Front. And I think that the origin of these problems is similar.

In one article, FHAR states that differences between the lesbian's situation and that of the faggot are not yet clear. And in *Faggotry*, a magazine put out by a group of New York effeminists, there is the following statement: "Many faggots have left the Gay Liberation Movement because even the most radical and militant factions have made a one-sided attack against sexism. Faggots have left Gay Liberation because they have seen male supremacy as the root from which all other oppressions branch." (About two years of struggle separate these two statements.)

During the early years of the Gay Liberation Movement in the U.S., faggots and lesbians—without the help of the two-hundred-year-old precedent which buttresses bourgeois liberalism—led an excruciating search for an ideology or set of principles which could serve as some sort of guide. At first it was thought that we simply had to integrate the question of gay liberation into the already existing mass

of Marxist-Leninist dogma, within the context of the straight-male revolutionary movement in the U.S. The impossibility of the task, together with the lack of a comprehensive analysis, was responsible for the tensions that grew within GLF and that eventually destroyed it. From what I've read, that seems to be pretty much where most of the men in FHAR are at right now.

Upon the ashes and ruins of the GLF in this country, some have begun building "Revolutionary Effeminism"—a movement which is becoming increasingly widespread and which has begun, using the insights of radical feminism as a foundation, to deal with some former GLF problems: "We are what is feared most: effeminists. Men who are struggling to become unmanly, men who oppose the hierarchy and ideology of a masculine fascism that requires that domination of one person by another, of one sex, race or class by another. We will become gentle but strong faggots who will fight their oppression in militant ways, faggots who are vulnerable to each other, able to cry, but not passive or paralyzed in our struggle to change."

In France, the impact of radical feminism has not yet been as strong as it has been here (they have a lot of problems that we don't have). And until very recently, the voice of radical lesbians from within the

FHAR hasn't been strong at all—in fact, they're still working with faggots. But just as things are beginning to move here, there are signs of change in France. A small group of people from within the FHAR (*groupe n° 5*) has begun putting out a newspaper called *le Fléau Social* ("The Social Plague"). In it, the voice of women and lesbians is much clearer, with titles such as "Smash Virility," slogans such as "Free Valerie Solanas," and an article attacking the youth-beauty ethic. In short, some of the questions are beginning to be answered.

The aforementioned article in *Faggotry* concludes by saying, "We are going to transform fields of vision exploding purple until there is a creation of a new reality organized during the nightbreaking sky." It took us a long time to get to this point, over two thousand years. So if it takes the FHAR a little longer, that's okay, it's an ambitious struggle. But for gay men right now, it's the only struggle.

part three

beyond
gay liberation

father knows best

I am gay and the father of three children. When I told my boys that I was gay, their first question was, "What does that mean?" I replied that it meant I prefer having sex with men. While at the time I congratulated myself for being so open with them, I think this answer was a disservice to them, to me and to my gay sisters and brothers. You see, I didn't help them come to a real understanding of who their daddy is. My answer was a shallow, sex-oriented explanation. Of course, there is a simple explanation for my answering in such a way: I couldn't help the children understand because I hadn't helped myself understand. I hadn't come to a real understanding of who their daddy is; I still have to work and struggle with what it means to say that I am gay.

I am at a place now where I am redefining what it means to be gay, and I can say without any qualification that I am not only proud to be gay, but I hope my boys will be gay.

I prefer sex with men, as I told my kids, but this is not the sum total of my gayness. Because the straight world didn't allow me a sensual relationship with men—only a handshake in public, a slap on the butt on the football field, an occasional hug at funerals, guarded conversations about personal feelings and one-upsmanship in business and sex; because the straight world wouldn't let me talk about my feelings of love for men and left me only an inner-directed fantasy world of absurd sex; because the straight world forced my love-making underground (and into dark bars, regularly raided bushes and smelly toilet stalls), I was brainwashed into thinking that my gayness was a sexual obsession and, sure enough, *that is what it was!*

When I came out I did the whole T-Room (public toilet) Trip with foot-tapping and "what do you like to do" note-passing. If I saw a face over the stall I would really freak out—all I wanted was an impersonal hand, mouth or dick. And I hated myself for it. *That* kind of homosexuality I don't want for my kids!

Later I met a guy who could enjoy sex with a person, not just a hand. So I played the game of late-hour visiting, the romance of a few stolen hours, and then back to the pretense of being straight in the light of day. Things were better, but I was asking my lover to revolve his life around a few hours in bed, while I had to act my life out of a guarded sham and much guilt. *That* kind of homosexuality I don't want for my kids!

So I came out in a really big way—separation and divorce, and a different trick every night. Man, was I free! All I had to worry about were those dry periods when I couldn't get a trick. And worry I did! Keep myself as butch as possible; hit the bars as often as possible; worry about my hair, my wrinkles and my charm. And *that* kind of homosexuality I definitely do *not* want for my kids! (Lest I sound too liberated: hair, waist, wrinkles, charm, butchness, bars and dry periods still plague me.)

Well, what *do* I want for my kids? Let me tell you about some of the feelings I had as a child.

I can remember a time when my friends —boys and girls—related on a more or less equal basis. I loved and was loved without reference to gender. We shared secrets and games, dolls and marbles, hurts and pleasures.

Then, slowly, attitudes began to change. Football was no longer something we played for fun; it was a competitive and physical way to prove maleness; it judged a boy by his ability to excel as an aggressor. I couldn't get into this and found myself separated from my brothers.

Sex was no longer the innocent pleasure it had been in childhood. From the older boys we learned that sex was conquest. Little Janie always sat in a certain corner of the movie house. Who was brave enough to get a feel? Everyone knew Barbara was an easy lay. Who would be man enough to try first?

It was the beginning of alienation of the sexes. Boys become masters over the soft little toys known as girls. Approval from the peer group was based on the success of "having my way" or "getting it on."

And I felt guilty when all of this repulsed me as a child. Because I felt more at home hanging around with girls, I thought something was wrong with me.

Hell, no! There was nothing wrong with me; there was something dreadfully wrong with my brothers. They were losing what I call their gayness and were moving into that sickness I call the straight world. And it has nothing to do with who one has sex with. It is the attitude that a man's tool makes him superior to women. It is the attitude that a man's relation to another man is aggressive and competitive. If a man shows emotion, that is a female weakness. If he gently caresses a brother's hair, he is suspected of being somewhat less than a man. And, my God, if he touches his brother anywhere between waist and knee, he is sick!

Bullshit! The gay man recognizes the oppression of women and strives to erase the prejudices which stand in the way of relating to them as equal beings. The gay appreciates the softness that should be a part of all men. The gay man gives up his privileged position of power and glories in his femininity. Gay women and men touch and trust. That's what I want for my boys!

But it may be too late. One of my sons had an illness which was almost fatal. As a result he has to wear special stockings all the time. He couldn't go to the bathroom at school this past year because the booths didn't have doors and the other guys made fun of his "women's stockings." He is dreading this next year, when he will have to take gym. He is ridiculed because he has to wear a garter belt to hold up his stockings. What kind of hell is that to put a kid through?

Another of my sons has a slight eye problem. His depth perception is poor so that it throws his coordination off and he can't catch a baseball as well as the rest of the guys. Do you know the anguish such a little thing can cause? It isn't enough for his mama and daddy to remind him that he is a fantastic reader. It isn't enough that we, his parents, can see the beauty of his sensitive nature. His peers have already made him doubt his worth.

Why in God's name must they go through

such needless hurt and self-doubt? Why? Because this society of ours is ruled by the sick values of *butch*: hail the conquering hero—watch me flex my muscles—see what I have between my legs.

Don't ask me again why I want my boys to be gay.

Postscript: After talking this article over with my sisters and brothers, I have decided to add the following:

The reason for my abruptness at the end was the rage I felt as the realization began to hit me harder and harder that my children are being pressured into a stereotyped image of maleness that kills their innate sensitivities. I also felt the pressure of the straight world that had forced me to think I had no alternative but to live apart from the boys, denying what I had to give them and what they had to give me. (It goes without saying that this also applies to the society-encouraged barriers between my ex-wife and me.)

I know that these three boys need the support of a gay-identified society. They need the identity of fully realized humanity —the "strength" that enables a man to fight tyranny and oppression; the "weakness" that allows a man to empty himself for another; the "sharpness" that motivates him to drive a sword into the injustices and inequities of today's power structures, the "softness" that gives him the force to reach out and comfort his sisters and brothers.

Pretty words and idealistic hopes? As a gay brother and father, I'm ready to struggle so that words and hopes become concrete realities for everyone—and especially for three boys I know.

harold norse
i'm not a man

I'm not a man. I can't earn a living, buy new things for my family.
I have acne and a small peter.

I'm not a man. I don't like football, boxing and cars.
I like to express my feelings. I even like to put an arm
around my friend's shoulder.

I'm not a man. I won't play the role assigned to me—the role
created by Madison Avenue, *Playboy*, Hollywood and Oliver Cromwell.
Television does not dictate my behavior. I am under 5 foot 4.

I'm not a man. Once when I shot a squirrel I swore that I would
never kill again. I gave up meat. The sight of blood makes me sick.
I like flowers.

I'm not a man. I went to prison resisting the draft. I do not fight back
when real men beat me up and call me queer. I dislike violence.

I'm not a man. I have never raped a woman. I don't hate blacks.
I do not get emotional when the flag is waved. I do not think
I should love America or leave it. I think I should laugh at it.

I'm not a man. I have never had the clap.

I'm not a man. *Esquire* is not my favorite magazine.

I'm not a man. I cry when I'm unhappy.

I'm not a man. I do not feel superior to women.

I'm not a man. I don't wear a jock strap.

I'm not a man. I write poetry.

I'm not a man. I meditate on peace and love.

I'm not a man. I don't want to destroy you.

Tony de Rosa

paul jacobs
what do you mean i'm prejudiced?

It was a typical Berkeley academic cocktail party in 1971: a handful
of distinguished elder professors in conservative dark or tweed suits,
at whose sides hovered their dispirited wives, ancient victims of
the male professor cult, mingling with a larger cluster of middle-aged,
almost-as-distinguished professors, some of them sporting mod haircuts
to match their mod sports coats and slacks. Their victim-wives stood
or sat scattered around the room talking desultorily with each other,
while on the outskirts of the party a few younger instructors and
graduate students were honored by being asked to drink with
the models for their own future. And since this was 1971, two major
topics of conversation drifting around the room were women's liberation
and sexual freedom. Then, despite frowns from the elderly professors
and their wives, the middle-aged savants began to demonstrate
their sexual liberation by discussing, determinedly and grimly,
fellatio and cunnilingus.

"There's one aspect to fellatio I never thought about until women's liberation brought it into my consciousness," I said, venturing into the dry and impersonal conversation. "Like every other boy, I learned from what I heard on the streets and in school that my cock would be like iron when it got stiff. All the phrases connected with it had that same sense . . ."

(The word "cock" obviously caused some uneasiness in the hitherto serious academic ambiance surrounding the conversation because I felt a disturbance around me, a nervous shifting from side to side as people looked at each other to gauge how they should react.)

". . . of hardness. You got a 'hard-on' or you had a 'stiff prick' and you were going to 'ram' your 'rod' into some girl who was lying there panting, just waiting for your 'steel' spike to come into her . . ."

(By now, the group around me was in an acute stage of discomfort, anxious and queasy, moving away from me as quickly as politeness would allow.)

". . . and so, being brought up to believe this all my life, it was a hell of a shock to me the first time I had a cock in my mouth and discovered how soft it was even when it was hard."

That did it. The room suddenly stopped. Movement and conversation ended, simultaneously, in a sudden painful silence. They looked at me as if I had just pulled down my pants and dropped a giant turd in the middle of the room. A few minutes later my wife and I left. We haven't been asked back.

The reaction of the academics and their wives to the notion of my sucking cock was typical of those whose views must be considered the most liberal in the straight world. Everyone in that room would favor changing laws which proscribe homosexual acts between consenting adults; every one of them knows at least one homosexual, male or female; every one of them approves of homosexuals fighting for their legal rights. And probably every one of them makes a disapproving moral judgment about homosexuality.

It was that disapproval which was so manifest in the shocked reaction of the group to what I had said. And added to their sense of outrage that I should have even said what I did so openly must also have been a feeling of fright, a sense of threat to themselves and their own orderly, structured vision of their own sexual-political personalities.

That emanation of fright is far more apparent when the straight world must deal not with homosexuals describing their homosexual experience, but with heterosexuals involved, in any way, in homosexual experiences or feelings. It is as if such heterosexuals have sold out, gone over to the other side, betrayed their class or religion or ethnic group. And linked to the notion of betrayal may be the nagging concern that if one heterosexual, no different in surface behavior from other heterosexuals, can find stimulation and satisfaction in homosexual acts, then all heterosexuals might be equally open to those feelings.

Certainly my explicit observation about how soft the hard cock felt in my mouth went far beyond the acceptable pattern of discussion in most of the straight world. Ordinarily, the heterosexual blocks out such visions even in fantasies (perhaps especially in fantasies). Suppose a man whose eyes were closed while his cock was being sucked opened them to see that the mouth enclosing him was that of another man; suppose a woman wriggling delightedly while a tongue worked its way around her clitoris discovered that it was another woman bringing her that joy—they could be psychologically destroyed, at the very least badly upset and disturbed. The sexual mores of the technological Western world, capitalist or communist, forbid thinking about such notions.

Should the straight world be thrown off balance? Should the gay world force such questions into the straight consciousness? Or should gays direct their attention to fighting for their own right to be open about their sexual identity and not suffer any penalties for it?

I don't know the answer to these questions; I haven't thought enough about them. Perhaps, too, I'm fearful that if I do consider them seriously, I might end up in a place where the homosexual experience would end at a level much different from simply sucking another man's cock when the man and the mood match.

I guess I'm not so liberated either.

Morris Kight (left) and Ralph Schaffer (center) represent gays at welfare demon-
stration/Los Angeles

ralph schaffer
will you still need me when i'm 64?

Gay Liberation has covered a wide terrain, geographically and
intellectually. We gay people have recognized our oppression,
and in different ways we are dealing with it. We are also confronting
our racism and our male chauvinism toward women and
each other. We are coping with gender identities and gender
chauvinism. At hundreds of Gay Liberation meetings in four cities
I have quietly raised my voice to speak of the "youthism" of gay
life—the chauvinism of people (young and old) against the older
gay male. People listen and move on to the next topic.

Now I'm beginning to get a little pissed. I think it is about time
Gay Liberation came to grips with its "youthism." It is the most
vicious and entrenched of our fuckups left over from our oppression.
It is tragic because it leaves half our gay people lonely, alienated
and unwanted.

Youthism is the unconscious belief that older people are inferior. We older gay men are looked upon as inferior in appearance, attractiveness, intelligence, and sexual prowess. Many of us have unwittingly accepted our alleged inferiority. Consequently, we cannot relate to other gay men our age—we must pursue the eternal eighteen-year-old Adonis.

Young people constantly use us. They use us to get a crash pad, to get money, food, jobs, contacts—and in return they condescend to let us do them.

All the aims and goals of Gay Liberation are for young gays. Nothing is for older gays—not even those who are hip and in the movement. The young take our contributions for granted, blithely accept the advantages (draft counseling, crash pads, etc.), drop a quarter in the bucket, smile, and wave good-bye. I'm not saying they should lay us in return. They should *serve equally.*

Who is an older person? Well, I remember two sweet young guys complaining to me at a Gay Liberation dance that some dirty old man was bothering them. The ''dirty old man'' was twenty-four years old! (And why is it that when an older man cruises, he's dirty?)

We hear a lot about the gay spirit, a spirit of a special tender love. Where is it? How can you speak of such a thing when millions of gays over thirty are lonely, isolated, rejected, unloved and unwanted! In gay life we must learn to relate to each other as human beings.

I have nothing against the older man who digs younger guys, or vice-versa—yes, there are some younger guys who really dig older men—but when an older man is so fucked up that he can't respond to a man his own age because he's got his eye on every sixteen-year-old, he's sick.

Why is he after the sixteen-year-old? Because he believes the physical beauty of youth is superior to the physical beauty of older men. Phooey. I'm in better shape at forty-two than many young fellows I've seen. The oppressed older man even believes he is not as beautiful as he once was. Nonsense. If our heads were not fucked up, we would see that not all older men are pot-bellied and bald. And so what if a guy does have a pot belly? A pot belly has its own kind of beauty, if you look for it. So do baldness and gray hair and wrinkles.

The older man has a beauty that is inaccessible to youth. His life story is written in his body, in his gestures, in his facial expressions. His body is the history of victories and defeats, moments of joy and moments of sorrow. We've had them all. Every man has a story to tell about life. He has visited places and travelled roads the young have not yet imagined.

The young cannot be blamed for not seeing this beauty. But older gay men have no excuse for overlooking the beauty and attractiveness of their peers.

The young person who concerns himself with the lousy fate of older gays is planning for his future. But, of course, young people don't really believe they will someday be a hoary thirty-three years old! Believe me, it comes faster than you think.

I have quit Gay Liberation after being extremely active for a full year. In Gay Liberation I've known more gay people than in all my life. I have never been so lonely. What a tragic comment on Gay Liberation.

Gay Liberation is masturbation.

nick benton
don't
call me brother

The only revolutionary liberation for men in this society is gay liberation.

Having said that, I would go further to say that as a gay male one of the most oppressive terms which has been used on me in my life is the term "brother."

"Hey, there, brother, how ya doin'!" (Slap, slap) Pounding me on the back or on my ass, the straight man has always tried to include me on his team by seducing me with the term "brother."

Only since gay liberation entered my life have I begun to wake up to saying, "I am not your brother . . . I am not like you . . . I won't let you presume I'm straight like you."

So then I see a new newspaper called *Brother*.

My first reaction is, "Here we go again. The men are getting it together again. They're banding together again, calling each other brothers." This type of bonding is what men have done since the dawn of time. Our society, as it is, is a society of brotherhoods. We already live in a "homosexual" (same-sex-oriented) society in which the strongest bonds are between men, in which women are generally excluded, and effeminacy in males is the highest sin.

The Masons call one another "brother." So, I'm sure, do the KKKers, the boys on baseball teams, in the military, in all of our socially "homosexual" institutions. In all cases, the term "brother" means a bond among those with power, and death both to women and male effeminists.

And, now, men's liberation emerges with its newspaper called *Brother*.

Are the men getting together for another assault on women and gay men, only this time a far more subtle assault, one which, rather than employing sheer power, employs co-optation?

The paper talks about men's liberation, "calling for men to free themselves of the sex-role stereotypes that limit their ability to be human." It talks about the elimination of chauvinistic relationships with women and about overcoming fears of homosex-

uality. But as good as the content of these articles may sound, it's what they don't say that I'm sensitive to.

The one thing which males in this society fear the most, and are the most alienated from, is effeminacy. Effeminacy is synonymous with the loss of power, synonymous with what it means to be gay.

It is not threatening to males to talk about relating better to (their) women, or even, in a sexually free society, to talk about having an occasional homosexual experience. They can do that very easily without losing their male prerogative, the power bestowed upon them simply by being born male.

The only way they could lose that power would be through embracing effeminacy—through becoming gay themselves, as opposed to talking about gayness, accepting gays or even having an occasional homosexual experience while hanging on to their masculine image.

As long as men insist upon retaining that power, they are the enemy of women and powerless men popularly known as "queers."

Does men's liberation subtly but effectively insist on retaining that male prerogative power? That's the critical question I, as a gay male, ask. If it doesn't, then it's just another in the endless list of male-bonding trips which must be offed in order for women and gay men to be free.

I understand that when some of the *Brother* staff tried selling their paper on the streets, many people thought they were peddling a gay newspaper. That's good, because some of them at least experienced how it feels to be put down for being "queer."

I wonder what they said when they were accused of being "queer."

By the same token, the *San Francisco Chronicle* felt it was important to assure its readers in the opening paragraphs of a recent front-page article that men's liberation was not a homosexual organization. I have not heard men's liberation renounce that classification as a nonhomosexual organization.

I contend that any male who feels it essential to his self-identity to say that he is not gay is my enemy.

My oppressors are not only police who pound me over the head with billy-clubs in dark alleys, but also those "nice" men who slap me on the back and call me "brother," then quickly remove their embrace and keep themselves a million miles away. My oppressors are all men who insist on their "divine right" to male power in the presence of those of us—women and gay men—who have no such power.

If men's liberation is genuinely seeking not to be oppressive to women and gay men, I suggest that all men's liberation people wear "How Dare You Presume I'm Straight" buttons.

n. a. diaman
breaking the ice

I

all those men
　　　talking
　　　　about their fucking revolution
　　　　and the women
　　　　　　they are fucking
thinking they will win
　　　　by being men fucking
men fighting
　　　　unable to touch each other
unable to love
they have become machines
　　　putting it in and shooting
　　　　not understanding
the real revolution
　　　the turning around
the changes
　　　　　a cycle of love
knowing only
　　　how to put it in
　　　　putting in their fucking bullets
shooting their fucking masculinity
　　　putting in their
　　　　　fucking cocks

continuing their
　　　　fucking violence
　　unable to see beyond
the fucking barrels
　　　　　of their guns
still fucking
　out of frustration
　　　　the dreariness
　　of unimaginative lives
not thinking of
　　a real revolution
　but reacting to the old
　　　playing the same roles
living the same fucking lives
　　unwilling to create
　　　　a whole new world

II

all those fucking straight men
　　talking about
　　　　their fucking revolution
their fucking
　　　needing to be fucked
to understand the difference
　　　the other side

184

turning around
       a real revolution
they are afraid to
       touch each other
to be touched
       allowing love to penetrate
the walls
       they hide behind
       their masculinity
they need to
       give in to love
       to feel another man
inside of them
              to understand
the love
       or violence
       of that act
to give up their privileges
       their fucking
              white male privileges
no longer
       on the top
  the necessary training
for the change to come
       when women

                    will take power
              from their hands
                    an equal share
              of everything
this loving revolution
              is more difficult
than bombs
                    it will destroy
              the prison of their minds
                    III
all those fucking men
              still talking about
                    their revolution
       still fucking
              with the revolution
       still talking and fucking
should take that revolution
              and shove it
       up their ass
              until they learn
                    to love it
       up their ass
then let that
                    loving
              revolution come.

supermen
in g-strings

"Dealing honestly with our homosexual feelings" or "Coming to terms with our homosexuality" are frequent phrases in the current lexicon of men's liberation. What these expressions mean I don't know. There's a strain in women's liberation, of course, that adulates lesbianism. Women who know themselves as basically heterosexual sometimes announce, after a period of consciousness-raising, that they are "ready for a lesbian experience." It reminds me of people who close their eyes, hold their noses, and take a dose of castor oil because it's supposed to be good for them.

Maybe homosexuality is good for some people. But I'm pretty sure it's destructive, really damaging, for me.

When I was about thirteen I discovered physical culture magazines with pictures of weight-lifters in G-strings. In some obscure way, they seemed to be THE ANSWER. I used to study the supermen secretly while masturbating. It was very humiliating. I never told anyone about it. The next step was to recruit an eighth-grade classmate —a hairy, uncircumcised guy (like my father)—and try to masturbate him. He couldn't get it up. I somehow sensed that handling his dick wasn't quite it.

So I went back to studying pictures. I had this humiliating habit, to a lessening degree, for years (now I'm thirty-three, married, the father of two). It periodically numbed me. In college I once tried to "deal honestly with my homosexual feelings" by making it with a gay man (he blew me). My attitude was, "Why not, if he wants it so much?" After, I think I said, "There now, I hope you feel better," as if I'd given him a dose of Pepto-Bismol. As for me, I felt like used shit. That's as depressed as I've ever been. It lasted about a week.

Why do I consider all this "humiliating"? I don't think it's because I was so unliberated that anything deviant was an automatic bummer for me. I did a lot of stuff that horrified my strait-laced family. I think what was so humiliating about my supermen-in-G-strings scene was that it fit in perfectly with the kind of crippling relationships my family had to offer. It seemed a sort of self-mutilation, a knuckling under, in obedience to certain strictures.

For example, when I was still very young, my mother forbade me to touch my penis. When I was three I was told, "When you were little, we had some skin cut off your penis, so you mustn't touch it or you might open up the cut." My mother used to give me dolls, and women's clothes to dress up in. Later she'd rage at me, after I did something that seemed effeminate to her, "You should have been born a girl." My bigger sister liked to beat me up and call me a sissy. The most painful, prolonged spanking I ever got was administered by my mother when she found me, my friend, my sister, and another girl—all of us between seven and nine—exposing ourselves to each other in our attic.

My father wasn't around much. He was a hard worker and a "good provider." He was much praised by my mother. He and I had two personal conversations that I remember. When I was eleven he told me not to "play with" myself because my penis "has to produce a seed." When I was fourteen he told me not to masturbate because it would cause dizzy spells.

Now, looking back, it seems as if supermen-in-G-strings were the answer because I was no kind of man at all in my own opinion. So I'd moon over heroes who were clearly qualified for sex. Somehow I got my unworthy rocks off while concentrating on them.

Even now, if I have a homosexual fantasy, it's something like this: I fuck the super-handsome, super-built, super-hung guy in the ass. I somehow merge with him. Then he or I balls some forbidding, demanding chick. Or I simply eat, that is, literally gobble up, bones and all, some super-macho specimen, rather like people who eat lions' hearts or warriors' livers to acquire the enemy's coveted characteristics. The important thing is that either I already have these characteristics or they don't matter. And balling guys certainly won't get them for me.

Being homosexual, for me, would mean accepting put-downs. Not that I don't unconsciously accept these masculinity put-downs anyway, to a degree, even if I don't make them the basis for my lifestyle. After getting married I started doing calisthenics. Now I swim forty laps several times a week. If I see a guy at the pool who is better looking, better built, or better hung than I, I sometimes get that old, fascinated, adoring, humiliated feeling. This may trigger a merge-with-him or a gobble-him-up fantasy. It all seems so steeped in self-hatred and sex-in-the-head, though, that I can't see it as the cornerstone of a good life.

A few weeks ago a guy in my men's group was talking about how he and another man he grew up with were really intimate. They'd shared a lot by talking and doing things together. And they'd both gotten to feel that some kind of physical intimacy would be good too. Maybe so, for them. Their experience is quite different from the homosexuality I feel in myself. Only remote, idealized, slightly contemptuous idols turn me on. Once I get to know a guy, no matter how well endowed he might be, I stop being aroused by him. A human being with smells, or quirks, hopes and fears, has nothing to do with my homosexual trip. I seek out gods, vessels for untrammeled fantasy. I lay my maleness on their altars. I get back a headful of nonsense about incomparable prowess and similar shit.

So men's liberation, and my men's group, has been an anti-homosexualizing experience for me. For guys like me, the movement can erode an inclination to worship other men, to see them as James Bond, or Muhammad Ali or Jimi Hendrix or any other super-macho, intimidating, unapproachable ideal.

pvt. dick johnson

sexism
in the new army

Last December (1971), ten thousand basic trainees at Ft. Ord,
California, boarded buses going home for Christmas leave. As
the groups of green-clad youths assembled for departure, news
photographers clustered around them, anxious to film "the beginning
of a sentimental journey." Each throng of soldiers hailed the newsmen
with uplifted arms, fingers shaping the familiar V. At Christmas, these
"boys in uniform" had a disturbing message for America: get out
of Vietnam. Today the Army is composed of soldiers of a new type
who in countless casual ways spout out "fuck the Army" and
who don't much care who is disappointed or irritated by the sentiment.

One reason the antiwar movement has been able to win popular support among the soldiery is for an analysis which says that the objective role of the Army is the protection of American corporate interests, and not "the defense of democracy," as the government would have people believe. Radical and pacifist ideas hold sway in the barracks. Those few soldiers who voice support for the war are ostracized by their fellows, and "okay dudes" badmouth the war and the government from top to bottom. Vietnam or Stateside, the story is the same: Short-term soldiers are fed up with militarism. Given this state of affairs, the perplexing fact is that somehow, the war continues; somehow, the military manages to train and use young people for its purposes. Despite their generally antiwar outlook, most soldiers do as they are told. The antiwar movement has been unable to generate a sustained wave of GI resistance to the Army, because it has failed to understand the subjective forces which make the soldier obey, perform, and fight.

The movement's error has largely been one of assuming that since patriotism is the official justification for the war, soldiers must still be attached to patriotic myths or else they would cast down their arms. But the truth is that patriotism is already dead, even among most career sergeants ("lifers")

and officers. The subjective role of the military is not the confirmation of a soldier's patriotism, for patriotism has lost its meaning. Instead, the Army confirms the soldier's manhood, and this is what motivated him to cooperate despite his political skepticism about the war. American soldiers know that their homes and hearths are not endangered by "Charlie Cong," but they feel that if they reject the military, by refusing to enter it or by opposing it from within, their masculinity will be placed in question. As one private remarked, "There's no way of knowing if a pacifist is really opposed to war or if he's only a coward." Demands of the male ego take precedence over considerations derived from an analysis of international politics.

The military establishment is, of course, wise to the temper of its troops. In creating the New Army, it has practically shelved anticommunism as a motivating mythology, but smartly retained the male-supremacist rewards for which "the service" has always been known. The incoming recruit is not told to "sound off like you're an American"; today's soldier would laugh at that. Instead, the exhortation is "Sound off like you've got a set of balls." Bayonet instruction may be punctuated with the following chant: "Men, what is the spirit of the bayonet?"

"To kill, drill sergeant." "Men, will you kill?" "Yes, drill sergeant." "Men, why will you kill?" "Because we have balls, drill sergeant."

Soldiers who file applications for discharge as conscientious objectors are no longer harassed with such questions as "What are you, some kind of Commie?" Instead, the query is "Are you some kind of pussy or something?" The Army's propaganda films still pay lip service to "the struggle against world communism," but the more effective content is delivered in such lines as "In Vietnam, you'll be able to find a way out of no way, to do what you thought could not be done." Vietnam becomes the conflict in which the soldier expects to prove, not that America is just, but that he is mighty, resourceful, invincible, "able to do a man's task in a man's world."

Five years ago radicals were regarded as "alien subversives" by their NCOs and officers. The newer attitude is revealed by the following incident. During a "shakedown inspection," drill sergeants discovered a small cache of revolutionary literature in a soldier's locker. Their comment on the discovery was, "Soldier, you read a lot. But not the right kind of stuff, you ain't got no fuck books." The sergeants viewed him not as a traitor to his nation, but as a traitor to his sex. His offense against Army mores was not that he neglected to read patriotic literature—no one does—but that he failed to interest himself in the literature of male dominance.

Nor can the Army's practice of homosexual exclusion be traced to any patriotic origins. Alexander the Great and a large proportion of his troops practiced homosexual love. In the New Army, radicals may be discharged; homosexuals always are. One suspects that homosexuals are discharged and women exempted from the military because their presence in great numbers would contradict the effectiveness of the prevailing chauvinist mythology.

The Women's Army Corps serves the Army in two ways. Objectively, WACs are nurses and secretaries. Subjectively, they are part of the negative side of motivation mythology. For example, soldiers must periodically pass a physical fitness test which includes a one-mile run. Before the race begins, male soldiers are usually warned, "We've got WACs who can run the mile in seven minutes, so you men should be able to do it in six." The prediction is usually disproved, but the male soldier tries harder to fulfill it because the accusation of femininity hangs over his head.

Traditionally, the troops have been taught to believe that "all WACs are either whores or lesbians," and both designations are disapproving ones in the soldier's vocabulary. But, since the effective mores of the Army are changing, one now hears a new insult as well: "All WACs are 'gung-ho'; after all, they volunteered for the service." The real causes of WAC enlistments are usually poverty and the oppressiveness of family life. Most WACs enter the service to escape tyrannical parents, "the customary age of marriage," and ghetto life, not to glorify the flag. Male soldiers sympathize with other males who join to escape the police, paternity suits, and a future as unskilled or uneducated workers, but their reasoning does not cross sex lines. The antiwar movement has anticipated the new insult. In the past few years, several groupings opposed to the war have encouraged young men to join the Army for the purpose of agitating inside it, but no such organization has encouraged young women to join the WACs. Conducting missionary work inside the armed forces is probably a poor idea, but not one whose positive aspects can be refuted by resort to chauvinist misconceptions.

If John Wayne spoke for the soldiery fifteen years ago, he no longer does. The ranks are sick of patriotism. If John Wayne was respected for personifying "balls" and the flag, only his balls hold attraction today. This circumstance reflects the strength of the antiwar movement in one sense. Imperialism now commands less influence over its soldiers than it formerly did. But this victory is not enough: the system has been able to "take care of business" in Vietnam (and elsewhere) despite the decline of patriotism.

The Vietnamese and other victims of the war cannot care much why American soldiers continue to bear arms against them. But if the struggle against imperialist military intervention is to continue gaining ground, the antiwar movement will have to take the role of sexism in the New Army into account.

william burroughs
sexual conditioning

Sexual morality in the Western world is based on the Bible and especially on the teachings of St. Paul, which attempt to impose the standard of sexual behavior for all people everywhere and forever. These teachings are now dead and unworkable. Dead since the pill has separated sexual pleasure from reproduction. Dead since overpopulation has made reproduction something to be curtailed rather than encouraged. Dead since experiments have shown that sexual desire is a matter of stimulating certain brain areas and that such stimulation is *purely arbitrary*. Admittedly, homosexuals can be conditioned to react sexually to a woman—or to an old boot, for that matter. In the same way, heterosexual males can be conditioned to react sexually to other men. And who is to say that one is more desirable than the other?

The latter-day apologists of St. Paul who call themselves psychiatrists and sociologists have nothing to recommend them but their bad statistics. Here is Dr. Charles W. Socarides in a letter to *Playboy* (June 1970):

"Five hundred million years of evolution have established the male/female standard as the functionally healthy pattern of human sexual fulfillment. . . ."

The human species is not more than one million years old, according to the earliest human remains so far discovered. Other species have had a longer run. Three hundred million years have established a big mouth that can bite almost anything off and a gut that can digest it as a functionally healthy pattern for sharks. Several million years established large size as functionally healthy for dinosaurs.

What may be functionally healthy at one time is not necessarily so under altered conditions, as the bones of discontinued models bear silent witness. But sharks, dinosaurs and psychiatrists don't want to change.

The sexual revolution is moving into the electronic stage. Recent experiments in electric brain stimulation indicate that sexual excitements can now be produced at push-button control. Experiments in autonomic shaping have demonstrated that subjects can learn to control these responses and reproduce them at will, once they learn where the neural buttons are located. Just decide what you want to be excited by and your local sex adjustment center will match your sex waves and provide a suitable mate of whatever sex while you wait. It is now possible to provide every man and woman with the best sex kicks he or she can tolerate without blowing a fuse.

Any candidate running on that ticket should poll a lot of votes and bring a lot of issues right out into the open.

① By the year 2000 the world that we live in was in a terrible state. People covered the Earth like ants, and there was hardly any room to sit down any more!

THE ANSWER TO OVERPOPULATION IS GAY LIBERATION!

⑤

I'LL SECOND THAT!

QUEER WE DIDN'T THINK OF THAT BEFORE

YA, BE FRUITFUL, DON'T MULTIPLY!

And all of a sudden, heterosexuality was against the law, and heterosexuals were something to be whispered about. !!!

⑧ And they had to make love in dark corners, and in the bathrooms at Greyhound Bus Stations

And so, the purge began. Heterosexual bars were raided, and hundreds of straights were taken away and locked up for lewd conduct.

young and old, were marching.

LOVE AND LET LOVE

(14) Ha, ha, ha, look at those freaks!

Ya, they probably do it with animals too.

And soon everyone, everywhere was allowed to do their own thing. And for the very first time love prevailed, instead of laws...

And everyone loved, happily ever after.

© Nov 1970 L. Richmond

199

allen ginsberg

at the
conspiracy trial

At the Chicago Conspiracy Trial, Prosecutor Thomas Foran, attempting
to prejudice the jury against my testimony protesting ''Spiritual High
Intentions'' as motive of ''conspiracy'' for public assemblage for redress
of grievances in Chicago 1968, asked me to read to the jury
a series of poems from my books *Empty Mirrors* and *Reality Sandwiches*
which he deemed might shock the jury with manifest faggot animality.
The following conversation concluded his cross-examination.

Allen Ginsberg
September 6, 1972

FORAN: You wrote a book of poems called *Reality Sandwiches**, didn't you?

GINSBERG: Yes.

FORAN: In there, there is a poem called "Love Poem on Theme by Whitman." Would you recite that to the jury?

GINSBERG: "Love Poem on Theme by Whitman," Walt Whitman being one celebrated bard, national prophet. The poem begins with a quotation of a line by Walt Whitman. It begins with the Walt Whitman line:

I'll go into the bedroom silently and lie down between the bridegroom and the bride,

those bodies fallen from heaven stretched out waiting naked and restless,/arms resting over their eyes in the darkness,/bury my face in their shoulders and breasts, breathing their skin,/ and stroke and kiss neck and mouth and make back be open and known,/ legs raised up, crook'd to receive, cock in the darkness driven tormented and attacking/roused up from hole to itching head,/bodies locked shuddering naked, hot hips and buttocks screwed into each others'/and eyes, eyes glinting and charming, widening into look and abandon,/and moans of movement, voices, hands in air, hands between thighs,/hands

* San Francisco: City Lights Books, 1963

in moisture on softened lips, throbbing contraction of bellies/till the white come flow in the swirling sheets/and the bride cry for forgiveness, and the groom be covered with tears of passion and compassion,/and I rise up from the bed replenished with last intimate gestures and kisses of farewell—/all before the mind wakes, behind shades and closed doors in a darkened house/where the inhabitants roam unsatisfied in the night/ nude ghosts seeking each other out in the silence.

FORAN: Would you explain the religious significance of that poem?

GINSBERG: As part of our nature, as part of our human nature we have many loves, many of which are denied, many of which we deny to ourselves. He said that the reclaiming of those loves and the becoming aware of those loves was the only way that this nation could save itself and become a democratic and spiritual republic.

He said that unless there was an infusion of feeling, of tenderness, of fearlessness, of spirituality, of natural sexuality, of natural delight in each other's bodies, into the hardened, materialistic, cynical, life-denying, clearly competitive, afraid, scared, armored bodies, there would be no chance for spiritual democracy to take place in America. And he defined that tenderness between the citizens as, in his words, adhesiveness, a natural tenderness flowing between all citizens, not only men and women but also a tenderness between men and men as part of our democratic heritage, part of the adhesiveness which would make the democracy function: that men could work together not as competitive beasts but as tender lovers and fellows.

So he projected from his own desire and from his own unconsciousness a sexual urge he felt was normal to the unconscious of most people, though forbidden, for the most part, to take part.

Walt Whitman is one of my spiritual teachers and I am following him in this poem, taking off from a line of his own and projecting my own actual unconscious feelings, of which I don't have shame, sir; which I feel are basically charming, actually.

THE COURT: I didn't hear that last word.

GINSBERG: Charming.

FORAN: I have no further questions.

biographical notes

LEN RICHMOND and GARY NOGUERA: Len is a 29-year-old film-maker. He made a documentary of the Los Angeles Gay Liberation Front, has worked for KQED Educational Television in San Francisco, and made some award-winning animated films. He grew up in Whittier, California. Gary was born and raised in New York City. He moved to California in 1970 and began compiling this book soon afterward. He has traveled to various parts of the world, including India as a follower of Avatar Meher Baba. At 21, he is a cross between a burnt-out New Yorker and a California nature child. Len and Gary met at a Gay Liberation Front meeting in San Francisco in 1970 and have been together since. They have been involved in gay politics in Berkeley, Los Angeles, London, and San Francisco. Len and Gary are lovers (but not in a monogamous, role-playing way). They now live in Mill Valley, a small town just outside San Francisco, with their dog Tony (who is also gay).

GARY ALINDER: "I grew up on a Minnesota farm and went to the University of Minnesota. Later I lived in New York City, where I was a shitworker at *Harper's Bazaar*. I then became involved in the peace movement and Lower East Side community organizing. I cruised Christopher Street, but only came out when I moved to California and became involved in gay liberation and the publishing of *Gay Sunshine* (1969-71). I am now a San Francisco cab driver/retired radical looking for something (someone?) new."

DENNIS ALTMAN is the author of the recently published *Homosexual/Oppression and Liberation* (New York: Outerbridge & Lazard, 1971). A native Australian, he teaches American Politics at the University of Sydney.

NICK BENTON: "Biographies are part and parcel of our oppression. To write one would fuck over my mind and my life. It would have nothing to do with who I am and where I'm actually at now. There can be some value in recovering one's past in order to understand it, and then surpass it and move beyond it, but generally nostalgia is a bad trip.''

KONSTANTIN BERLANDT: Born in San Francisco, he was at one time the editor of the *Daily Californian* (University of California, Berkeley). He later became an important activist in the early gay liberation movement in San Francisco and Berkeley and was one of the editors of *Gay Sunshine* (1969-71). He has recently returned from Israel, where he spent some time living on a kibbutz. Now back in San Francisco, he is wondering, ''What happens next?''

PERRY BRASS: ''I was born in Savannah, Georgia, where I came out at sixteen. After a year at the University of Georgia, I realized that southern society was a vicious, conscious plot against women, blacks and gay men. I came to New York City, where I joined the Gay Liberation Front in 1969. I believe that the gay liberation struggle means being able to express the full range of my feelings and learning consciously not to oppress myself or others. It also means learning to give up male privileges in a very sexist society.''

WILLIAM BURROUGHS: Born in St. Louis, Missouri, he is the author of *Naked Lunch, Nova Express,* and other books. He now lives in London.

N. A. DIAMAN is a member of New York City's Gay Revolutionary party and one of the editors of its magazine, *Ecstasy.*

ARTHUR EVANS is one of the founders of New York's Gay Activists Alliance. His book, *The Oppression of Homosexuals,* should be published shortly.

ALLEN GINSBERG: ''Ommm.''

PAUL GOODMAN is the author of *Growing Up Absurd* and many other books. He died in Hawaii of a heart attack shortly before this book went to press.

PATRICK HAGGERTY lives in Seattle, Washington, and is an ex-member of the Venceremos Brigade.

JOEL HALL lives in Chicago, where he was a founding member of Third World Gay Revolution.

RALPH HALL: ''I was born a human sensualist in South Glens Falls, New York, in 1945 and turned out faggot (the only way for males to be. To struggle and survive = faggotry). I was one of the many who experienced the Gay Liberation Front in New York City as it was, and who lived to tell about it. I wrote about GLF (the movement's movement) and self in *Gay Power, The East Village Other, Gay Sunshine, Come Out,* and I now publish *Faggots and Faggotry,* an anarchist mimeo-paper directed towards men.''

DON JACKSON became involved in gay liberation in Los Angeles. He now lives in San Francisco, where he writes regularly for *Gay Sunshine* and *The Advocate*.

PAUL JACOBS: A movement reporter and journalist, he ran for U.S. Senate in California on the Peace and Freedom party ticket.

DICK JOHNSON is a pseudonym for a private stationed at Fort Ord, California.

LOUIS LANDERSON has worked extensively in Berkeley and Boston gay politics. He now writes for Boston's *Fag Rag*. (All translations in his article are his own.)

JOHN LENNON is married to the famous Yoko Ono.

STEP MAY: "I grew up on a chicken farm in South Jersey, then studied linguistics at the University of Chicago. I was active in GI organizing in the South and in the student radical movement when gay liberation started. After several months of non-stop faggotry, I decided to go to Cuba with the third Venceremos Brigade and I was in the first Venceremos Brigade gay caucus. Now I'm active on the Chicago Gay People's Legal Committee and I hope some day to practice law in a red dress."

HUEY NEWTON is one of the founders of the Black Panther party.

HAROLD NORSE: A New Yorker who spent many years in Europe and Morocco, he now lives in San Francisco, where he edits his poetry magazine *Bastard Angel*. He says, "Gay liberation and human liberation are the same thing."

RALPH SCHAFFER: One of the founders of the Los Angeles Gay Liberation Front, he was later a member of the Gay Liberation House Commune and then the Los Angeles Gay Community Service Center. He was shot and killed on August 27, 1972, in an apparent robbery of the Gaywill Funky Shop in Los Angeles, which he managed.

GORE VIDAL is the author of *Myra Breckenridge* and other books.

ALAN WATTS is the author of *The Book, The Way of Zen*, and others. He works closely with the Esalen Institute and lives in Mill Valley, California.

ALLEN YOUNG: The son of struggling Jewish communist chicken farmers, he grew up in the Catskill mountains. He is the co-editor, with Karla Jay, of *Out of the Closets: Voices of Gay Liberation* (Douglas Books, 1972). He was a stringer for the *New York Times* and later a staff writer for the *Washington Post*. He quit the *Post* to join Liberation News Service and then helped start the Seventeenth Street Collective and worked on its street paper, *Gay Flames*. He now lives near Boston with four friends.

photo credits